Signs of Life

Signs of Life

Sermons and Meditations

Gerd Theissen

SCM PRESS LTD

Translated by John Bowden from the German
Lebenszeichen. Predigten und Meditationen, published
1998 by Christian Kaiser/Gütersloher Verlagshaus,
Gütersloh.

0 334 02757 8

First published 1998 by
SCM Press Ltd
9–17 St Albans Place London N1 0NX

Typeset by Regent Typesetting, London
and printed in Great Britain by
Biddles Ltd, Guildford and King's Lynn

Contents

Contents

Preface

'Signs of life' is a phrase that we use when after a long time we hear from someone with whom we had lost contact. We weren't quite certain whether he or she was even still alive. Modern sermons are signs of life in this sense, messages about someone whom many people believe to be already dead yet who keeps getting in touch through the barriers put up by our everyday mentality. Sermons are signs of God's life. The 'signs' that they communicate are enigmatic. The very derivation of these 'signs' is open: they're not just signs of God but signs of life in us which has not yet 'died out', despite all assertions to the contrary. They are signs of life around us – messages from the whole of creation, which is far more than those parts of it that we can exploit. But above all they are signs of the life of other people, people whom we avoid because the signs of their life often disturb us and unsettle us.

These signs of life are enigmatic because they are often to be found in the offensive, the immoral and the absurd. If we look for them in the Bible, we find them in anger about the wickedness of the world, in the immoral readiness of a father to sacrifice his son – and in the intrigues of a son against his father and his brother. If we look for them in the present, we come up against the relics of a love which is still alive in everyday quarrels, or the discussion of Jews about the night of the Holocaust. These are signs of life between the burning thorn bush and the crown of thorns – recalcitrant, alien and alienating. There is often nothing edifying about them in the traditional sense; they seek to demonstrate the absurd theatre of this world in order to give strength to resist the absurd.

But they remain enigmatic even when they have delivered their message. Their message is meant to make contact with God possible – contact with a mysterious and enigmatic reality.

In the Bible they are accompanied with a prohibition against making images. But precisely because material images of stone and wood are excluded, linguistic imagery flourishes all the more vigorously in the Bible: here God is not just father and mother, not just friend, beloved, spouse, but also robber, enemy and oppressor, fire and storm. However, at one point God even abandons all this linguistic imagery with his aniconic 'I am who I am.' This central sign of God's life interlocks with signs of human life wherever men and women are enabled to say 'I am who I am' – sovereign in the face of social control and in solidarity with all those who similarly can say 'I am'.

Sermons are not dialogues between individuals. They are addressed to a community. They depend on the expectation of that community that biblical texts expounded in a lively way are an opportunity for entering into dialogue with God. Granted, many centuries separate the communities of today from those of the New Testament, but in some respects the two come close together – and not just in size, minority status and pluralistic environment. None of that is decisive. Paul once described the New Testament community as a sphere in which the separation between Jews and Christians, slaves and free, man and woman, is overcome (Gal. 3.28). Here he is describing the three tensions which are also 'signs of life' for a living Christianity in the present-day community.

In the last few decades the relationship between Jews and Christians has undergone a far-reaching revision. Judaism is being re-evaluated not only as the historical mother religion of Christianity but also as a contemporary partner in dialogue. It is being experienced by an increasing number of Christians as a 'sign of life' from God. Its traditions, experiences and reflections are given equal rights in Christian discussion of God and the world.

Slaves and the free do not confront one another in our communities. But there are differences of rank and status, possessions and power everywhere. These sermons reflect the change in social climate in European societies which became universally evident at the latest after the major economic shift in

1992. They offer no solutions to the contradictions of a society which has to be far more profit-orientated in its economic calculations and can no longer rely on non-profit-orientated solidarity in dealing with the social consequences of economic developments. But they strongly express the conviction that the command to serve life applies to all spheres of life and that a social conscience cannot retreat from politics and economics.

Finally, they reflect the relationship between man and woman. Some people want to suppress this theme again in the face of growing economic difficulties and increasing unemployment. So far the churches have resisted the temptation to join in here and to restore the conservative models of the man-woman relationship which they once advocated. There is no mistaking the fact that living communities everywhere are shaped and supported by women, even if women are nowhere near being appropriately represented in church governments. The unrest which stems from feminist perspectives is one of the most powerful signs that faith is still alive today.

Anyone who doubts the future and the viability of a gentle form of Christianity will find such 'signs of life' today where the dialogue with Judaism is again being taken up, where social tensions challenge the conscience, and women and men redefine their relationship. As in earliest Christianity, a living spirit is kindled at these points. But it has to be conceded that for many people these signs of life are still 'enigmatic'. These sermons seek to decipher such enigmatic signs of life, to interpret them as signs which provide courage for living and believing.

I am grateful to all those who have indirectly shared in shaping my sermons by their critical response, above all my wife. And I want to thank Petra von Gemünden and Annette Merz for critically reading the written versions, Annette Weissenrieder for her editorial work on them and for reading the proofs, Heike Goebel and above all Helga Wolf for providing a series of revised texts until the final version was achieved.

Heidelberg, September 1997   Gerd Theissen

Anger as a Sign of Life

or Abraham's intercessions for Sodom and Gomorrah

(Genesis 18.16–33)

Then the men set out from there, and they looked towards Sodom; and Abraham went with them to set them on their way. And the Lord thought, 'Shall I hide from Abraham what I am about to do, seeing that Abraham shall become a great and mighty nation, and all the nations of the earth shall bless themselves by him? No, for I have chosen him, that he may command his children and his house-hold after him to keep the way of the Lord by doing righteousness and justice; so that the Lord may bring to Abraham what he has promised him.' Then the Lord said, 'Because the outcry against Sodom and Gomorrah is great and their sin is very grave, I will go down to see whether or not they have really done what is claimed in the outcry which has come to me.' And the men turned from there, and went towards Sodom; but Abraham still stood before the Lord. Then Abraham drew near, and said, 'Will you really destroy the righteous with the wicked? Suppose there are fifty righteous within the city; will you then destroy the place and not spare it for the fifty righteous who are in it? Far be it from you to do such a thing; to slay the righteous with the wicked, so that the righteous fare as the wicked! Far be that from you! Shall not the Judge of all the earth do right?' And the Lord said, 'If I find at Sodom fifty righteous in the city, I will spare the whole place for their sake.' Abraham answered, 'Behold, I have taken upon myself to speak to the Lord, I who am but dust and ashes. Suppose five of the fifty righteous are lacking? Will you destroy the whole city for lack of five?' And he said, 'I will not destroy it if I find forty-five there.' Again he spoke to him, and said, 'Suppose forty are found there.' He answered, 'For the sake of forty I will not do it.' Then he said, 'Oh let not the Lord be angry, and I will speak. Suppose thirty are found there.' He answered, 'I will not do it, if I find thirty there.' He said, 'Behold, I have taken upon myself to speak to the Lord. Suppose twenty are found there.' He answered, 'For the sake of

1

twenty I will not destroy it.' Then he said, 'Oh let not the Lord be angry, and I will speak again but this once. Suppose ten are found there.' He answered, 'For the sake of ten I will not destroy it.' And the Lord went his way, when he had finished speaking to Abraham; and Abraham returned to his place.

We can understand this story if now and again we are angry at the whole world – so angry that we think that it really deserves to be destroyed. Of course we will be horrified at such an aggressive thought. How can one react so primitively, so sweepingly, in such an un-Christian a way to the wickedness of the world? How can one show such unrestrained moral aggression?

Yet I confess that sometimes I have such an un-Christian anger in me. And I have an ally for my anger in the Bible – in the story of Abraham's intercession for Sodom. For this story tells us that God himself is angry at this world. We heard about his great anger earlier: 'The Lord saw that the wickedness of human beings was great in the earth, and that every imagination of the thoughts of their heart was continually evil. And the Lord was sorry that he had made human beings on the earth, and it grieved him to his heart. So the Lord said, "I will blot out humankind whom I have created from the face of the ground . . ."'

Why do I sometimes find these sombre words comforting? They comfort me because I think: if God is so angry at human wickedness, then as God's image I too can confess to having such anger. Certainly I can't put myself in a very good light, since I'm one of those human beings with whom I'm angry. I must also be angry with myself. But anger isn't logical; it's just there.

Anger comes over us in two forms. It comes over us as anger at the great inhumanity of war and political catastrophes: anger at soldiers and generals in Bosnia who fire on hospitals, rape women, carry on cease-fire negotiations and proclaim truces, simply to gain time to seize more territory. Anger at the Sudanese authorities who murder their own people, the Sudanese Christians in the south. Anger at those Germans in the generation before us who ran a great murder factory in a hitherto unprecedented way.

And then there is another variant of this anger – anger at the petty everyday inhumanities. What emerges in war and genocide as organized human wickedness is less obvious in the trivial everyday wars which do not have such devastating consequences. But it's the same evil. Anger comes over me when someone loses a good reputation through gossip, when goodwill is blatantly refused or a readiness to help is shamelessly exploited. Anger comes over me when people are systematically harassed and humiliated. As I've said, it's the same person who wages the big wars – and who stands out in the little everyday wars.

Dear people, confess that you too are also sometimes just as angry! Then you will be as full of life as the God of the Bible – a God who is angry at human wickedness. In this way anger can become a sign of life. Those who are angry aren't completely dead. Those who are angry haven't yet become resigned. Those who are angry still have the strength to resist.

Once we have conceded our anger in this way, we can listen to Abraham. Abraham negotiates with God, but at the same time he negotiates with us. He goes about it skilfully. He doesn't criticize this anger for being so primitive. This divine anger is no more selective than our anger. It treats good and evil alike. It's sweeping and unjust. Nevertheless, Abraham doesn't say, 'Lord, simply be angry with the wicked and reward the good. That would be discerning. That would be cultivated. That would be fair.' No, Abraham says, 'If your anger means that many righteous people have to suffer because of a few villains, why shouldn't it be the other way round? Why shouldn't your joy at a few righteous people benefit the many villains?' Abraham wants to activate the primal violence with which God wants to annihilate everyone because of a few villains so that God preserves everyone for the sake of a few righteous people. He wants to use this primal, primitive violence which is so sweeping for a good purpose.

And what about us, we who are images of God? Can we too transform our sweeping anger into such goodness? Abraham

3

tells us that fifty righteous are enough. Abraham negotiates with us: forty-five would do, or perhaps even forty or thirty or twenty – in the end it's down to ten righteous people. Ten should be enough for us to overcome our great anger at the world for their sakes, to accept the world despite everything.

Now of course we make our retort. 'Abraham, you've a kind heart. You presuppose ten righteous people. But there aren't that many. People in our humane days don't like to be told, but the fact remains that human wickedness is great on earth. All the devices and desires of our hearts are evil. That's shown by the big wars and the petty everyday skirmishes.'

Yes, there are evil abysses in any human heart, and the great anger at the wickedness of the world further confirms that. For it does an injustice to many people. It puts them all in a bad light. It doesn't differentiate. It indicates an abyss of aggression in the human heart.

But when this great anger comes over me – anger at the world which is always also anger at God, because God created this world – when I cry out to God in despair, 'Why did you make me at all and hurl me into this muck?' – then in the end I think of just one person, for whose sake I should and can give up this anger. There is just one righteous man whom many regarded as unrighteous – just one man: Jesus of Nazareth. If this one person has lived in our world, then I may no longer reject the world, annihilate it and destroy it in flights of the imagination, and add to all the violence it experiences the violence of my unrestrained, excessive moral aggression. If God turned his anger to love for the sake of this one man, shouldn't I at least be able to desist from my anger?

When I was younger, I felt this anger even more intensely than I do now. At that time I wrote a short poem about Jesus. Instead of saying in abstract terms why Jesus leads me to give up my anger at the world, I shall end with this poem. Not because I think it aesthetically valuable, but as a testimony to the one man Jesus of Nazareth.

Among so many figures
you too have a place.
Myths and legends
disguise your face.

Tortured, a failure,
you hang on the cross;
priestcraft and politics
led to your loss.

Your painful presence,
suddenly there,
casts a strange spell
on the world that we share.

Strange fascination
with suffering and pain,
anger, disgust at
how much is in vain.

If you are silent,
who can cry,
if there abandoned
you're left to die?

You, its hidden pain,
often hard to see.
Words cannot fathom
your mystery.

This sermon was given on 18 May 1994 at the Wednesday morning service in St Peter's Church, Heidelberg. The war in Bosnia was at its height. The inability to end it or at least to prevent the excessive violations of human rights and war crimes in it was (and is) a trauma for all those who believed human beings to be capable of peace. I wrote the poem quoted at the end towards the end of my theological studies in the 1960s – not least under the impact of the Vietnam war, to which we reacted just as angrily as to the war in Bosnia today, though with an optimism that in principle such wars could be avoided. Today we have lost this optimism.

God's Terrible Experiment

Abraham on Mount Moriah

(Genesis 22.1–18)

*After these events God tested Abraham, and said to him,
'Abraham!' And he replied, 'Here am I.' God said, 'Take your son,
your only son Isaac, whom you love, and go to the land of Moriah,
and offer him there as a burnt offering upon one of the mountains
of which I shall tell you.' So Abraham rose early in the morning,
saddled his ass, and took two of his young men with him, and his
son Isaac; and he split the wood for the burnt offering, and arose
and made his way to the place of which God had told him. On the
third day Abraham lifted up his eyes and saw the place afar off.
Then Abraham said to his young men, 'Stay here with the ass; I and
the lad will go over there and worship, and come again to you.' And
Abraham took the wood of the burnt offering, and laid it on Isaac
his son; and he took in his hand the fire and the knife. So they went
both of them together. And Isaac said to his father Abraham, 'My
father!' And he said, 'Yes, my son.' He said, 'Here are fire and
wood; but where is the lamb for a burnt offering?' Abraham said,
'God will provide the lamb for a burnt offering, my son.' So they
went both of them together. When they came to the place of which
God had told him, Abraham built an altar there, and piled the
wood on it, and bound Isaac his son, and laid him on the altar,
upon the wood. Then Abraham put forth his hand, and took the
knife to slaughter his son. But the angel of the Lord called to
him from heaven, and said, 'Abraham, Abraham!' And he said,
'Here am I.' He said, 'Do not stretch out your hand to the boy or
do anything to him; for now I know that you fear God, seeing you
have not withheld your son, your only son, from me.' And
Abraham lifted up his eyes and looked, and behold, behind him was
a ram, caught in a thicket by his horns; and Abraham went and
took the ram, and offered it up as a burnt offering instead of his
son. So Abraham called the name of that place Yahweh yireh ('The
Lord sees')'; as it is said to this day, 'On the mountain the Lord
shows himself.' And the angel of the Lord called to Abraham a*

second time from heaven, and said, 'By myself I have sworn, says the Lord, because you have done this, and have not withheld your son, your only son, I will indeed bless you, and I will make your descendants as numerous as the stars of heaven and as the sand on the seashore. And your descendants shall possess the gate of their enemies, and by your descendants shall all the nations of the world bless themselves, because you have obeyed my voice.'

Anyone who listens to the story of the sacrifice of Isaac without being indignant is morally blind. Anyone who despises it as a relic of inhumane times is in an even worse state: such a person is blind, yet claims to see.

God performs a macabre experiment on human beings. It resembles another experiment which was performed in the name of science. The subjects were young students, young men and women whose moral sense is usually not too worn down. They were told that the experiment furthered research into human attitudes to pain. They were taken into a room where they were to use a keyboard which generated electric currents; another, invisible person was exposed to these in a neighbouring room. First came low-voltage currents, but these were steadily increased. This caused cries in the neighbouring room which grew louder and louder. The person in charge of the experiment assured the students that they need take no notice; it was all in a good cause. He asked them to raise the voltage higher and higher by pressing buttons – and the cries in the neighbouring room became more and more unbearable. Only a few stopped the experiment. Most were prepared even to inflict fatal charges.

What those involved in the experiment did not know was that the cries in the neighbouring room were simulated. Nor did they suspect that what was being tested was not human attitudes to pain but their readiness to abandon moral inhibitions for allegedly higher ends – to the point of even having no inhibitions about killing. They were being tested – not others.

My question now is: What is the moral difference between Abraham being tested by God and this experiment? Isn't the Old Testament God of Abraham more merciful than the modern director of the experiment? Doesn't he intervene before Abraham kills? Nevertheless, in both cases we have a macabre experiment. And in both cases the gain in knowledge is that human beings can be led to kill, especially if an appeal is made to higher values, to religion and science.

So I can well understand why the story of the sacrifice of Isaac has disappeared from the religious education curricula. But is that a reason for removing it from the canon of our church (and our culture)? Should we remove it from the list of sermon texts which are prescribed for this Sunday? Or should we reformulate it? Suppose a commission were appointed to look into these questions. Four experts will be invited. At the end the commission will formulate its own verdict on the sacrifice of Isaac.

The first expert is a scholar of religion. He says: 'The story is more humane than it might appear to be at first sight. It is intended to ensure the abolition of child sacrifice for all times. The temptation to sacrifice children came from the peoples who were Israel's neighbours. There was child sacrifice in Moab and Phoenicia – especially in times of crisis and emergencies. The Israelites had to ask themselves: do we worship our God less than our neighbours worship theirs if we are not prepared to give up what is dearest and most precious to us? To justify their attitude they told the story of Abraham. They meant it to convey that Israelites, too, were prepared to give up everything. However, fortunately God was content with the intention to do this. God doesn't require the cruel offering of human sacrifices. On the contrary, God thwarts it. God forbids it. The God of Israel is more humane.

The commission finds much to think about here. This clarifies the historical background to the story. But there is agreement that in the story itself the test isn't imposed by the neighbours. In the story it is imposed by God himself.

The next expert to appear is a philologist. He offers a solution which he found in a rabbi. God didn't say to Abraham 'Offer your son', but 'Make him go up' (viz. up the mountain). Abraham misunderstood. He heard the word *olah,* burnt offering, but what was meant was a form of *alah*, go up. It was all a mistake on Abraham's part.

The commission thought that while this proposal might have been convincing to Rabbi Acha, who made it, in history it is not human stupidity which imposes the test; God does.

The third expert is a philosopher from the town of Königsberg. For him it is clear that when one hears a voice which is contrary to the moral law, this cannot be the voice of God. What he actually says is: 'Abraham should have said to this allegedly divine voice, "It is quite certain that I should not kill my good son; I'm not completely certain that you are God, nor would that be clear even if the voice were to resound from a visible heaven."'

The commission finds this convincing. But it goes on to ask: is the test in the story simply imposed by a false image of God? Isn't it imposed by God himself?

The last expert to be heard is a woman theologian. First of all she says precisely what is expected of her. 'The story of the sacrifice of Isaac is a typical male story. There isn't a word about Sarah. Abraham is alone with his servants and with Isaac. Sarah's absence is the problem. Some rabbis already felt this. Immediately after the sacrifice of Isaac Sarah is mentioned one last time in Genesis. She dies. "Why?", the rabbis asked. Their explanation was that when Sarah heard upon Abraham's return what had happened on Mount Moriah, she fainted and died. Understandably. What wife would want to go on living with a husband who was prepared to slaughter their child?'

Some members of the commission want to cut short this obligatory statement of feminist theology. But our expert has another idea. She says: 'There is often talk of the voice of God in history. First of all it commands Abraham, "Sacrifice your son." The second time it appears as the voice of an angel from heaven which says, "Do not stretch out your hand to the boy or do anything to him." Here we have the phrase "stretch out the hand to someone" which elsewhere (e.g. in Ps.125) becomes "stretch out the hand to evil". Now what is the decisive difference between the voice of God at the beginning of the story and the voice of the angel in the middle? At the beginning God himself says, "Go and sacrifice." That is the sacral language of the cult. But the angel calls this sacral sacrifice a wicked act. He says, "Do not do anything wicked to the boy." That is the language of ethics. One could almost wish that it was the other way round and that the angel gave the command to sacrifice Isaac at the beginning. After that, God would intervene to take back the inhuman command of a subordinate authority. Then one could say that here a false picture of God was being corrected by the true God. But that isn't the case. It's precisely the other way round: God's own voice is corrected by the angel! But who is this angel? What is interposing itself here between God and human beings? This angel speaks of God in the third person: "Do not do anything to the boy, for now I know that you fear God." This angel is distinct from God. He contradicts God. He is not simply God's messenger. But in that case, who is he? If one could retell the story today in a women's Bible, it would sound something like this. Sarah had had an inkling of Abraham's dark intentions. She had hurried ahead of him. She had tied up a ram in a thicket and hidden herself there. She was the one who at the decisive moment had cried out, "Do not stretch out your hand to the boy or do anything to him." The voice of the angel was the voice of Sarah. But of course that isn't in the story. It's been read into it. Yet even in its present form that leaves a gap. Where is Sarah in it? Hasn't the angel given the absent mother a voice? Wasn't the voice of the angel which spoke within Abraham in fact the voice of Sarah in him, the voice of the wife and mother who has been suppressed from the story? Didn't this voice arise out of Abraham's unconscious? And isn't that why for him it came from heaven?'

Some members of the commission want to adopt this solution. But the women members in particular have their doubts. This solution is too simple for them. If only the men (and the errors of theological male fantasies) were the problem, they would be quite happy. But in the story the test isn't imposed by males, but by God.

There is a long discussion. Finally the commission comes to a conclusion. The key to the story is to be sought at the beginning and the end. At the beginning it is said that this is a test, a temptation of Abraham. That's a signal to the listener: look out – there's a temptation. Perhaps on first hearing you think that Abraham is being tempted. But in reality you're being tempted. In reality hearers and readers are being put to the test. But what is their temptation? What is being tested?

That emerges from the end of the story. There the angel renews the promise of blessing to Abraham. God will give him many descendants: 'By your descendants shall all the nations of the world bless themselves, because you have obeyed my voice.' This is where we, those who listen to and read this story, are introduced. For we too belong among the peoples who should wish for a blessing in the name of Abraham. What test are we being subjected to here? What is our temptation?

There are two possible ways of understanding the conclusion. We are told that Abraham will be blessed because he has listened to the voice. Does it remain open which voice is meant? That's deliberately left ambiguous, like so much in this story, as ambiguous as Abraham's announcement that God himself will provide a lamb for sacrifice. Now we're being tested about which possibility we shall choose.

The first possibility is that the voice being referred to is that of God at the beginning, the language of the cult, which says, 'Sacrifice your son.' Abraham's test would be whether he was prepared to do this. When Abraham says to his son, 'God will provide a lamb for sacrifice', he knows that God will provide Isaac. Abraham thinks, 'Perhaps God is inhuman, but just as he gives life, so too he has the right to take life.' Therefore Abraham is ready to kill his son for the greater glory of God.

The other possibility is that the voice being referred to is that of the angel, the voice of ethics, which says, 'Do not do this wicked deed.' Abraham is blessed because he followed this second voice. Abraham is blessed because he did not blindly obey the first voice to the bitter end, but listened to the voice which intervened like a mother to save the child from death.

And earlier, on the way to Mount Moriah, he hoped for this voice. When he says to his son, 'God will provide a lamb for sacrifice', he trusts that God will provide something other than Isaac – even if this is at the very last moment. For God has promised him descendants through Isaac. This promise holds, even when everything tells against it. So from the start Abraham trusted in God's humanity. He trusted that God wants life and not death.

Those of you who have chosen the second version have passed the test. But in the long history of reflection on the sacrifice of Isaac, most people have chosen the first version – though with changes, so that one cannot say that none of them has passed the test. It is usually said that Isaac offered himself voluntarily. Jews saw prefigured in Isaac their readiness for martyrdom – a martyrdom which God required of them time and again. At the same time Christians and Jews said that Abraham offered Isaac in faith in the resurrection. He trusted that God could bring him back from death to life.

I know of only one person who chose the second version in an early period, Paul. In Romans he appeals to Abraham as the great model of the faith which God reckons for righteousness. He makes two changes to the usual interpretation.

The first is that for him Abraham becomes godless. Abraham believed in the one who justifies the godless; in the one who forgives sins. I keep asking myself: what sin is Paul thinking of? Is Abraham perhaps one of the godless for him because he was ready to slaughter his son? But that's only a question!

The second change, however, is clear: Abraham's righteousness does not consist in the sacrifice of Isaac but in his faith in the promise of Isaac's birth. Abraham is righteous because he believes the promise that he and Sarah will have a son, although their capacity to father and bear a child was dead and spent because of their age. Here faith which justifies consists in a faith in the God who gives life – not in a God who calls for killing.

For me there is no doubt that Paul shrinks from seeing Abraham's exemplary faith in his readiness to kill. In so doing he contradicts the image of Abraham in his time – among Christians and Jews. What has happened here? How has it come about? In the case of Paul, too, a voice from heaven intervened! He was about to arrest some Jews who believed in Jesus (and it was said that he was ready to kill them). He too was prevented from this by a voice from heaven. But he didn't hear an angel. He heard Jesus himself – before Damascus: 'Why do you persecute me? Why do you want to put the knife to the throat of children of Abraham?' Here too a mediator figure between God and humankind intervened – not an angel, but the Crucified and Risen One, through whom God seeks to make a covenant for life with all men and women: a covenant in which life finally has priority over death.

Abraham is not the only one who has to withstand a test. We all have to. Life is a great test to which we are subjected. We are all given apparently well-founded instructions to press buttons which cause pain to others. We all succumb to the temptation to sacrifice our children. The altars on which we sacrifice are not made of stone but of concrete. Mount Moriah is not shrouded with clouds but towers up into a gap in the ozone layer. The knife that we wield is technological progress. And we too are ready to sacrifice the future of our children in the name of higher values. But if we're attentive, we hear the shouts and cries of those who suffer and are tormented alongside us – in rooms which are cut off by filters.

We shall all be tested. When will we say, 'I refuse to go along with that'? When will we say no? But how difficult it is! Like Abraham, we have two innate dispositions: the readiness to kill and the readiness to resist death. The perplexing thing is that we cannot distinguish between the two as clearly as we would like. The voice of death and the voice of life lie confusingly close to each other. Indeed the same voice is sometimes the letter that kills and sometimes the spirit that gives life. In human hands the most sacred values can become a norm that kills, and the best philosophies can justify immorality. The most humane religion can pervert, and the religion of love become the breeding ground of hatred and fanaticism. That isn't because there are neighbours who do the wrong thing. It isn't just because of human stupidity, which doesn't understand holy traditions. It isn't because of antiquated pictures of God which Königsberg philosophy could dispose of. Nor is it just because of the patriarchal poison which is about everywhere. We must learn from Abraham that death and life lie so closely together that they can hardly be distinguished. We must learn from Paul that the God who first made him a persecutor was the same God who all his life dissuaded him from this madness.

Like Abraham and Paul, human beings are both sinners and righteous at the same time, *simul iustus et peccator*. They are beings full of a lust to kill and a love of life. It is precisely for that reason that the story of the sacrifice of Isaac is so necessary. It shows us that both the will to life and the will to death are in us. But life can conquer death. Abraham followed the voice of life and therefore was a righteous man, although there was the whole potential of a child murderer in him. Paul followed the call of Christ and therefore became a righteous man, although he had been a fanatical fundamentalist. If we too follow this voice – the same voice that Abraham heard in the Old Testament and Paul in the New – then the promise also applies to us. It does so, although there is a tremendous potential for murder in us. For not only soldiers but all human beings are (potential) murderers. But to all men and women (and to all soldiers) is given the promise that we have descendants on this earth – that a blessing lies upon the maltreated earth and peace and justice will fill it.

And may the peace of God which surpasses all our understanding keep your hearts and minds in Christ Jesus. Amen.

A sermon given in St Peter's Church, Heidelberg, on 24 March 1996. The experiment described at the beginning of the sermon is the Milgram experiment, which has now become a classic. It was performed by the Harvard psychologist Stanley Milgram (born 1933) in an investigation of extreme submission to authority. See S. Milgram,

God's Terrible Experiment

Obedience to Authority, New York 1974. The philosopher from Königsberg is of course Immanuel Kant. His comments on Gen. 22.1–18 quoted in the sermon appear in 'Der Streit der Fakultäten' (1798), in id., *Werkausgaben X, Schriften zur Anthropologie, Geschichtsphilosophie, Politik und Pädagogik*, ed. W. Weischedel, Frankfurt [10]1993, 261–393: 333. For the history of the exegesis of Gen. 22.1–18 see M. Krupp, *Den Sohn Opfern? Die Isaak-Überlieferung bei Juden, Christen und Muslimen*, Gütersloh 1995. Once the Federal Constitutional Court had declared the quotation from K. Tucholsky, 'soldiers are murderers', a legitimate expression of opinion, some government circles planned a law which would also make such statements an offence. The end of the sermon refers to this.

The Father's Longing for Sons

Isaac's blessing for shepherds and hunters

(Genesis 25.19–34; 27.1–45)

These are the descendants of Isaac, Abraham's son: Abraham was the father of Isaac, and Isaac was forty years old when he took to wife Rebekah, the daughter of Bethuel the Aramaean of Paddan-aram, the sister of Laban the Aramaean. And Isaac prayed to the Lord for his wife, because she was barren; and the Lord granted his prayer, and Rebekah his wife conceived. The children struggled together within her; and she said, 'If it is to be like this, why have I become pregnant?' So she went to enquire of the Lord. And the Lord said to her, 'Two nations are in your womb, and two peoples, born of you, shall be divided: the one shall be stronger than the other, the elder shall serve the younger.' When her days to be delivered were fulfilled, behold, there were twins in her womb. The first came forth red, all his body like a hairy pelt; so they called him Esau. Afterwards his brother came forth, and his hand had taken hold of Esau's heel; so his name was called Jacob. Isaac was sixty years old when they were born. When the boys grew up, Esau became a hunter, a man of the field, while Jacob was a civilized man, staying near the tents. Isaac loved Esau and liked eating his game; but Rebekah loved Jacob. Once when Jacob was cooking a meal, Esau came in from the field, and he was famished. And he said to Jacob, 'Let me eat some of that red dish, for I am famished!' (So his name was called Edom.) But Jacob said, 'First sell me your birthright.' Esau said, 'I am about to die; of what use is a birthright to me?' Jacob said, 'Swear to me first.' So he swore to him, and thus sold his birthright to Jacob. Then Jacob gave Esau bread and a dish of lentils, and he ate and drank, and rose and went his way. Thus Esau despised his birthright.

When Isaac had grown old and his eyes were so dim that he could not see, he called Esau his older son, and said to him, 'My son'; and he answered, 'Here I am.' He said, 'Behold, I have grown old; I do not know the day of my death. Now then, take your weapons, your quiver and your bow, and go out to the field, and hunt game for me, and prepare for me the kind of meal that I love, and bring it to me that I may eat; that I may bless you before I die.' Now Rebekah was listening when Isaac spoke to his son Esau. So when Esau went to the field to hunt for game and bring it, Rebekah said to her son Jacob, 'I heard your father speak to your brother Esau, "Bring me game, and prepare for me the kind of meal that I love, that I may eat it, and bless you before the Lord before I die." Now therefore, my son, listen to me and do as I tell you. Go to the flock, and fetch me two good kids, that I may prepare from them the kind of meal that your father loves. You shall bring it to your father to eat, so that he may bless you before he dies.' But Jacob said to Rebekah his mother, 'Behold, my brother Esau is a hairy man, and I am a smooth man. Perhaps my father will touch me, and I would seem to be deceiving him, and bring a curse upon myself and not a blessing.' His mother said to him, 'Upon me be your curse, my son; only obey my word, and go, fetch them to me.' So he went and took them and brought them to his mother; and his mother prepared the kind of meal that his father loved. Then Rebekah took the best garments of Esau her older son, which she had with her in the house, and put them on Jacob her younger son; and the skins of the kids she put upon his hands and upon the smooth part of his neck; and she gave the food and the bread which she had prepared into the hand of her son Jacob. So he went in to his father, and said, 'My father'; and he said, 'Here I am; who are you, my son?'. Jacob said to his father, 'I am Esau your first-born. I have done as you told me; now sit up and eat of my game, that you may bless me.' But Isaac said to his son, 'How is it that you have found it so quickly, my son?' He answered, 'Because the Lord your God granted me success.' Then Isaac said to Jacob, 'Come near, that I may feel you, my son, to know whether you are really my son Esau or not.' So Jacob went near to Isaac his father, who felt him and said, 'The voice is Jacob's voice, but the hands are the hands of Esau.' And he did not recognize him, because his hands were hairy like his brother Esau's hands. So he blessed him and said, 'Are you really my son Esau?' He answered, 'I am.' Then he said, 'Bring it to me, that I may eat of my son's game and bless you.' So he brought it to him, and he ate; and he brought him wine, and he drank. Then his father Isaac said to him, 'Come near and kiss me, my son.' So he came near and kissed him; and he smelled the smell of his garments, and blessed him, and said, 'See, the smell of my son is as the smell of a field which the Lord has blessed! May God give you of the dew of heaven, and of the fatness of the earth, and plenty of grain and wine. Let peoples serve you and nations bow down to you. Be lord over your brothers, and may your mother's sons bow down to you. Cursed be every one who curses you, and blessed be every one who blesses you!' As soon as Isaac had finished blessing Jacob, when Jacob had scarcely gone out from the presence of Isaac his father, Esau his brother came in from his hunting. He also prepared a meal and brought it to his father. And he said to his father, 'Arise, my father, and eat of your son's game, that your soul may bless me.' His father Isaac said to him, 'Who are you?' He answered, 'I am your son, your firstborn son, Esau.' Then Isaac trembled violently, and said, 'Who was it then that hunted game and brought it to me, and I ate it all before you came, and I have blessed him? – yes, and he shall remain blessed.' When Esau heard the words of his father, he cried out with an exceedingly great and bitter cry, and said to his father, 'Bless me too, my father!' But he said, 'Your brother came with guile, and he has taken away your blessing.' Esau said, 'Is he not rightly named Jacob? For he has supplanted me these two times. He took away my birthright; and behold, now he has taken away my blessing.' Then he said, 'Have you not reserved a blessing for me?' Isaac answered Esau, 'Behold, I have made him your lord, and all his brothers I have given to him for servants, and I have provided him with grain and wine. What then can I do for you, my son?' Esau said to his father, 'Have you just one blessing, my father? Bless me also, my father.' And Esau lifted up his voice and wept. Then Isaac his father answered him: 'Behold, away from the fatness of the earth shall your dwelling be, and away from the dew of heaven on high. By your sword you shall live, and you shall serve your brother; you shall break his yoke from your neck.' Now Esau hated Jacob because of the blessing with which his father had blessed him, and Esau said to himself, 'The days of mourning for my father are approaching; then I will kill my brother Jacob.' But these words of Esau her older son were told to Rebekah; so she sent and called Jacob her younger son, and said to him, 'Look, your brother Esau is threatening to kill you. So listen to me, my son; arise, flee to Laban my brother in Haran, and stay with him a while, until your brother's fury turns away and he forgets what you have done to him. Then I will send and fetch you from there. Why should I be bereft of you both in one day?'

Today many people lament the collapse of the family. If we read the stories about Jacob and Esau, we will be comforted: the family was always an almost impossible undertaking. Here one brother shamelessly exploits the hunger of another. A wife conspires against her blind husband. A brother has to flee to escape being murdered. What an impossible family! And yet it's all realistic: the conflicts of this family are meant to represent conflicts between peoples. The struggle between Jacob and Esau in the womb is the struggle of two peoples in Rebekah's body. Conflicts between peoples are in fact often as irrational as a fight between two embryos in the same womb. And if the family in the literal sense is an almost impossible enterprise, how much more is that true of the family of nations! Nowadays ethnic groups are raising their voices everywhere and are making life difficult for themselves – even if they have the same mother. Everywhere they are claiming rights over one another, exploiting every advantage, driving one another out. The drama of Jacob and Esau is taking place everywhere.

But in the Bible a great promise stands over this family drama: the promise to Abraham of land and descendants – not at the expense of other peoples, but for their blessing. The promise says, 'Through you shall all peoples on earth find blessing' (Gen. 12.3). To translate it in a different way: one day all peoples will wish one another blessings with you or with your name. Nowadays when ethnic groups pursue their promises of land and descendants, as a rule that means a curse for others; it means suffering, expulsion, inhumanity. Isn't it an unworldly utopia when at the beginning of the history of Israel with Abraham, i.e. at the beginning of the history of Jews, Christians and Muslims, we read the promise that through this one people all peoples will be blessed?

If we read the stories about the patriarchs, we get the impression that those involved aren't even aware of the blessing hovering over them when they act out their conflicts and engage in their intrigues. But suppose that they wanted to justify their action in the light of this promise of blessing – what would they say?

Let's begin with Rebekah and hear her justification. 'I know,' she says, 'that you regard me as a devious old woman who is led by irrational love of her youngest son to deceive her blind husband. Yes, I've grown old, among these men whose life consists first in hunting and eating and secondly in eating and drinking. And things would have gone on like that had I not taken the initiative. I watched them closely. Esau was the usual kind of man: hairy, impulsive, primitive. As a hunter he only knew how to kill. Jacob was more refined. Not just because of his smooth skin. He was a shepherd, someone who cherishes and preserves life. If a hunter doesn't have a catch for a long time he gets so starving that he falls upon anything edible. Success in hunting can't be planned. Getting a catch is a matter of luck. My Jacob's different. As a shepherd he knew that he always needed food. He had his flock around him. He could plan. But how could such a refined type stand up to the robust Esau? Was the chance happening that Esau was born before him to ensure Esau's pre-eminence for ever? What a primitive view! Someone sees the light of day first – and already thinks that everyone else must obey him, everyone else must fall in behind him. Had I not intervened, life would still be following these primitive rules. You may call it irrational mother's love. Isn't it better for such love to get involved in the distribution of opportunities in life than for the stronger automatically to get the upper hand? And how could I get by in this man's world, in which only the stronger win through, except through deceit? Yes, I helped the weaker one, Jacob, who was born second, with guile. And that's what culture is: helping the weaker – also against the strong. By guile, if there is no other way.' Thus Rebekah.

Esau argues the opposite case. 'Dear mother,' he says. (He really does say 'Dear mother,' since he is still very fond of her.) 'You are so incredibly shrewd that as your child I too must have also inherited something of your shrewdness. And this shrewdness tells me that you shrewd people play the same dirty tricks as we do. But with one difference. You often find fine words to present your dirty tricks as the promotion of culture. I don't do that. When I'm drunk, I say I'm drunk. When Jacob gets intoxicated he drivels on about a transcendental extension of consciousness. I'm too stupid for that. That's my fault. But I tell you, dear mother, once the whole world is dominated by you super-wise people, *we* shall become the weaker ones: we, the primitive, the coarse, the hairy. And then I doubt whether you will also apply your morality, that the weak have to be helped, to us. No, you won't do that. You'll get at us with your damned wisdom. And we'll be generous enough to take it all. Yes, my mother has really hit me, but I still love her. My brother has cheated me, but I'm still ready to be reconciled with him. So who has the higher culture here – you wise people with your transcendental consciousness or we primitive, good-natured fellows? Who have I cheated? Who have I deceived? Who have I exploited? Isn't my only failing that I'm different: rather hairy, rather primitive, rather awkward?' Thus Esau.

Now it's Jacob's turn. 'I accept that I cheated. I won't attempt to talk myself out of that. I've paid for it. Fourteen years' slavery abroad; twenty years' separation from the family. I too have experienced being cheated with false promises. But that doesn't alter the fact that I cheated you, Esau. However, both of us would find reconciliation easier if you too accepted that you also bore some of the blame. That first time, when you exchanged your birthright for a dish of lentils, I didn't cheat you. You rushed in and wanted something to eat, as usual. You scorned your father when you threw away your birthright. Getting something to eat when you were hungry, and getting it immediately, was more important to you than anything else, even your birthright. I only cheated you the second time. And that too is excusable. I simply put into practice what you showed me the first time: the principle that it's decisive to provide food as quickly as possible. That's *your* maxim in life. And I applied it to our old father. He wanted food. I, the shepherd, could get it for him more quickly than you could. I had animals available. As a hunter you didn't. According to your principles, I was better. If I as a shepherd can provide food more reliably, quickly and effectively – then by your standards I have the blessing. You had already promised it to me. Yes, in the longer term we shepherds really do have the greater blessing. We make it possible for more people to be fed despite the increasing scarcity of land on earth – through a more effective economy. The blessing which is there for all peoples lies on us. That it has been handed on by deceit casts a dark shadow. But something of this shadow also lies on you. Don't blame me for living by maxims which you showed me.'

But what does Isaac say to all this? Isaac has long suffered under the fact that he cannot bless both his sons. Why is any blessing limited? Why does the blessing for one means that it is withheld from the other? This question has always concerned him – even when he blessed the false Esau. Today he asks himself: 'Why did I bless this supposed Esau with words which apply neither to Esau nor to Jacob? I didn't wish the passionate hunter Esau prey in hunting. What I said was,

> May God give you of the dew of heaven,
> and of the fatness of the earth,
> and plenty of grain and wine.

That wasn't a blessing for a hunter. But it wasn't a blessing for a shepherd either. It was a blessing for farmers, for people who are neither hunters nor shepherds. And now I know why I did it. I suspected that the opposition between Jacob and Esau could be done away with and overcome only when the productivity of the soil was increased by agriculture. Only when there was enough for all, so that no one was any longer afraid of going short. So I dreamed of a life beyond the opposition of hunting and keeping flocks. Nevertheless the riddle remains. Why did I allow myself to be deceived so easily? Wasn't I almost certain that it wasn't Esau who was standing before me? Jacob was standing there. It was his voice. And then I touched him. I felt that it wasn't Jacob. It was Esau's skin. And I smelt his coat. It smelt of Esau. Nevertheless a voice said to me, 'Something's wrong.' How could Esau, the hunter, have got game for me so quickly? Why did it never occur to me that an intrigue was going on here? After all, I knew that Rebekah preferred Jacob, so that often I had to support Esau to keep the balance. I knew that my two sons were different. I knew of their hostility. They often quarrelled. But I loved them both: the rough and the smooth, the unkempt and the cultivated, the hunter and the shepherd. They were both my sons. Indeed, it was my secret longing for the good qualities of both of them to be combined in one person. And I experienced that when the crafty Jacob assumed the form of Esau. There were two persons in one: Jacob's voice and Esau's hair, Jacob's shrewdness and Esau's directness, Jacob's culture and Esau's natural style. The secret vision of my dreams came to me. No one deceived me, neither Rebekah nor Jacob. I allowed myself to be led astray by my own longing, my longing for a son who was both Esau and Jacob at the same time. I finally allowed myself to be led astray by the promise to Abraham: in you *all* peoples will be blessed: Jacob *and* Esau, Israel *and* Edom, the Jews *and* all others.

Now we've all heard voices from a broken family. But such broken families can be a place where the great dreams grow. People go on dreaming Isaac's dream. Centuries later, one of his descendants proclaims that now it has been fulfilled. Paul is writing to the Galatians. Now the blessing of Abraham applies to all peoples. For all those who are in Christ,

> There is neither Jew nor Greek,
> there is neither slave nor free,
> there is neither man nor woman.

In other words:

> There is neither Jacob nor Esau;
> one does not rule over the other.
> There is neither Isaac nor Rebekah;
> one does not cheat the other.
> There is neither hunter nor shepherd;

one does not have the advantage over the other.
You are all one in Christ Jesus.
You are all children of Abraham,
You are all heirs of the promise.

The tragedy of Jacob and Esau was that in their world only *one* could be heir of the promise. But Paul preaches that now *all* can be heirs of the promise and the blessing. How is that possible? Why is the blessing all at once no longer limited? It is unlimited because this blessing consists in the message that all are recognized unconditionally by God, regardless of their actions, their origin, their sex, their education. This message is a blessing for all. It is itself the blessing.

So can we say that a great promise is formulated in the Old Testament and fulfilled in the New? That's too simple. Let's think of Isaac, who allowed himself to be led astray by his longing for harmony between his sons, and who deceived himself because he thought that his longing had been fulfilled. Aren't we Christians similarly in danger of deceiving ourselves? Isn't the promise of a blessing for all peoples still unfulfilled? In reality, isn't it both fulfilled and unfulfilled?

We need a corrective so that we don't deceive ourselves by thinking that it has already been fulfilled. The Jewish rabbis provide such a corrective. For them Esau means Edom, and Edom means Rome. Rome has to live by its sword. Rome is the crude power which relies on its military might. The rabbis say that the conflict between Jacob and Esau has not yet been resolved. It has not been resolved as long as one people rules over another. But even rulers and ruled, the imperialistic peoples and those peoples who are subject to them, remain brothers. They come from the same womb. And over them both stands the same unfulfilled promise: one day all will be blessed.

The promise is both unfulfilled and fulfilled in Christ. Through Christ an unconditional will to recognize all men and women comes into our life – to recognize all men and women even when they are at enmity with God, with themselves and with others. This immaterial blessing can be shared infinitely.

But it is equally true that the promise has not been fulfilled in the world. Jacob and Esau still fight over the material blessing of this world, and that blessing cannot be shared infinitely.

Yet since Christ, something has changed. Not only Jews but also people from other nations now look to the fulfilment of the promise to Abraham. And in that fact something of this promise has already been fulfilled.

And even today, this very day, it can again be fulfilled: if, like Abraham, you believe that God will also make you a blessing for others, although so much tells against it.

You will object, 'Why should I in particular be a blessing for others? I'm far too weak or too gross, too young or too old, not ready or already worn out, too damaged by my environment or my job! Aren't we all happy when we get through life decently?'

But look at Isaac. Wasn't he old and blind? And yet a blessing came forth from him.

Look at Rebekah. Was she perfect? Yet she handed on a blessing.

Look at Jacob and Esau. Were they model brothers? And yet the blessing was active in their lives.

Look at the whole of this broken family. They were all damaged by their environment. And yet they were blessed.

If God makes such people the vehicles of his blessing, he can also do the same with you. And it all begins if you believe simply one thing of him: that he wants to recognize all men and women, unconditionally: the weak and the robust, the young and the old, the unready and the worn out, those damaged by environment or job. God wants to recognize all of them and make them all vehicles of his blessing, regardless of their qualities, their potential, their status and their education. He wants his blessing to be multiplied: his immaterial and his material blessing. And for that he needs normal people, people like Isaac and Rebekah, like Jacob and Esau. People like you and me.

And may the peace of God which surpasses all our understanding, keep your hearts and minds in Christ Jesus. Amen.

This sermon was given in St Peter's Church, Heidelberg on 25 June 1995. As one instance of the widespread identification of Edom and Rome see jTaan 4.8, fol 68d, a passage which refers to the fall of the fortress of Betar, the last bastion of the Jewish rebels in the Bar Kokhba revolt: 'The voice is the voice of Jacob and the hands are the hands of Esau (Gen. 27.22). The voice of Jacob cries out because of the misdeeds that the hands of Esau have done to him in Bethar . . . Rabbi Johanan said: "The voice of the emperor Hadrian kills 80,000 myriads in Bethar." '

I Am Who I Am

Signs of life in God between the burning bush and dogmas

(Exodus 3.1–15)

Now Moses was keeping the flock of his father-in-law, Jethro, the priest of the Midianites; and he led his flock beyond the wilderness, and came to Horeb, the mountain of God. And the angel of the Lord appeared to him in a flame of fire out of the midst of a bush; and when he looked, the bush was burning, yet it was not consumed. And Moses thought, 'I will go over there and see this marvellous sight, why the bush is not burnt.' When the Lord saw that he went over to the bush, God called to him out of the bush, 'Moses, Moses!' And he replied, 'Here am I.' Then God said, 'Do not come near; put off your shoes from your feet, for the place on which you are standing is holy ground.' And he said, 'I am the God of your father, the God of Abraham, the God of Isaac, and the God of Jacob.' And Moses veiled his face, for he was afraid to look at God.

Then the Lord said, 'I have seen the affliction of my people who are in Egypt, and have heard their cry because of their taskmasters; I know their sufferings, and I have come down to deliver them out of the hand of the Egyptians, and to bring them up out of that land to a good and broad land, a land flowing with milk and honey, to the place of the Canaanites, the Hittites, the Amorites, the Perizzites, the Hivites, and the Jebusites. And now, behold, the cry of the people of Israel has come to me, and I have seen the oppression with which the Egyptians oppress them. Come, I will send you to Pharaoh that you may bring forth my people, the sons of Israel, out of Egypt.' But Moses said to God, 'Who am I that I should go to Pharaoh, and bring the sons of Israel out of Egypt?' He said, 'But I will be with you; and this shall be the sign for you, that I have sent you: when you have brought forth the people out of Egypt, you shall serve God upon this mountain.' Then Moses said to God, 'If I come to the people of Israel and say to them, "The God of your fathers has sent me to you," and they ask me, "What is his name?",

what shall I say to them?' God said to Moses, 'I Am who I Am.'
And he said, 'Say this to the people of Israel, "I AM has sent me to
you."' God also said to Moses, 'Say this to the people of Israel,
"The Lord the God of your fathers, the God of Abraham, of Isaac,
and of Jacob, has sent me to you": this is my name for ever, and
thus I am to be remembered throughout all generations.'

Today is Trinity Sunday: the festival of the triune God. But who
knows what belief in the Father, the Son and the Holy Spirit is
all about? Who can still understand the existential questions
which led to this faith? And don't some of us also think that this
is an abstruse doctrine? Two scenes from past centuries, both
set in Heidelberg, can outline the problem.

In the first scene, we find ourselves in the market place in
Heidelberg in 1572, the day before Christmas Eve. There the
Reformed preacher Johann Sylvanus was executed before his
two sons for denying belief in the Trinity. He had doubts about
the divinity of Jesus. His execution was carried out, among
other things, at the instigation of the strict Reformed prince
Frederick, who was also called the 'Pious'. Other preachers who
had difficulties with belief in the divinity of Christ and the Holy
Spirit had fled. One of them, Adam Neuser, who had also been
pastor at St Peter's Church here at one time, escaped to
Constantinople, where he went over to Islam. Another fled to
Siebenbürgen. At one time belief in the Trinity was a life-and-
death matter.

The second scene, four hundred years later, is more peaceful.
It too takes place in Heidelberg, at my home. My son is about
to take his school-leaving examination in religion. The question
of God is one of those 'starred' topics for which everyone must
prepare. He has just been reading something about it once
again. At breakfast he asks me: 'There was also something
about the Trinity in it, all very obscure. Can you give me a quick
explanation?' 'How much time do I have?,' I asked. 'I've got to
go in five minutes.' Five minutes' brief instruction on the
doctrine of the Trinity – that's really impossible. But today I
would like once again to offer the answer I gave him then. I
said: 'You need to be clear that in thinking about God three

decisions were made in early Christianity – and three alternatives were ruled out.

The first decision was that God himself has created the world – not some subordinate demon, on whom one could foist all its imperfections. The temptation not to attribute the world to the good will of a Father of all things but to a bungler or a blind deputy god or a metaphysical accident was great. But people deliberately decided against that. God wants this whole world. It isn't the work of the devil. Therefore Trinity first of all means belief in God the Father, the creator of all things. In other words, it is belief that in principle the world is good. It isn't the product of the devil.

The second decision was that God doesn't prefer to keep a distance from the body with its needs and its limitations. Rather, God wants the whole person – with body, death and finitude. So God truly became human, in order that everything in human beings should be redeemed: nothing was to be left out. At that time people had a great temptation to limit God to something inner, higher and spiritual in human beings. In the face of this, it was finally decided that God became fully human. The whole person has been assumed by God. God wants the whole person. Therefore Trinity secondly means faith in God, the incarnate Son. In other words, human beings are worthy to be filled wholly by God. Nothing is left out: not even the body, not even death.

The third decision was this. As authoritarian powers, religion and church can require belief in their doctrines, regardless of whether these doctrines enlighten people or not. That was and is a timeless temptation. But there was a deliberate decision against such a view: it was said that God is present in every believer by his spirit. Assent to God and his will isn't something that is imposed from the outside. Assent comes from within. Like recognizes like. God's spirit in us makes God recognizable beyond us. Faith is faith only where it is based on inner evidence without any external constraint. God wants not only the human being, including the body and finitude, but also the free consent of the inner person through his Spirit. God brings this about in

the human spirit. Therefore, thirdly, Trinity means belief in God
the Holy Spirit. In other words, God wills the free assent of
human beings without any compulsion. God doesn't want any
authoritarian religion.'

My five minutes were up. I really should also have said something to my son about the doctrine of the 'immanent' Trinity.
For the origin of the doctrine of the Trinity was not just about
equal access to God through the world, human beings and the
spirit, but also about God's being in itself, even beyond his
manifestation to us. The 'immanent' doctrine of the Trinity says
that God also exists in himself (and not just for us) in a threefold way. But who these days would venture to ask school-
leavers in an examination about the doctrine of the immanent
Trinity? So before my son left I simply also told him quickly the
story of a heretic in Venice who was accused of heretical views
on the Trinity. Before the 'Council of Ten' he conceded that
while he understood God the Father and God the Son, he
couldn't understand the Holy Spirit. He wasn't condemned. 'He
understands at least two,' said the judges. 'We don't understand
any of them.' That makes one think. The Catholics in Venice
were more tolerant than the Reformed in Heidelberg, the
lawyers more worldly-wise than the theologians. So I let my son
go without having introduced him to the innermost mysteries of
belief in the Trinity.

In the evening I asked him, 'How did religion go?' He had in
fact been tested on his understanding of God: not, however, on
the Trinity of Father, Son and Spirit but on a far more earthly
trinity, on Feuerbach, Marx and Freud. He was tested on the
modern suspicion that God is merely a projection of human
beings: either an unconscious self-understanding about their
own nature or an illusory way of coping with tensions in
society or conflicts in the unconscious depths of the human soul.

When we investigate the trinitarian God today, we in fact
face two sets of questions: there are the questions from outside,
the penetrating questions of the criticism of religion, and the
questions from inside, the questions of John Sylvanus, the
questions of Muslims and Jews.

We also encounter these questions from within in our sermon text. Jews rightly understand it as testimony to a strict monotheism: the God of Abraham, Isaac and Jacob is only one. He is the one and only God, whose social partners are not other gods but human beings – and only human beings. God can be worshipped without images. Certainly there is much linguistic imagery in the Bible. God is father and mother, husband and lover, friend and tempter, but also enemy and robber, beast of prey and trapper, fire and storm. However, God leaves all this linguistic imagery far behind him when he reveals himself to Moses in the burning bush as 'I AM WHO I AM' or 'I WILL BE WHO I WILL BE'. That sounds abstract. But it is the greatest self-definition of God ever. God defines himself to us as I. God is not IT. God is an I, an I who has the power to determine and define himself. And this I first of all says only one thing about himself: I exist, live, today and tomorrow. I AM WHO I AM.

Wouldn't it be better if we limited ourselves to these statements and understood everything else (including trinitarian ideas) as sacred poetry, as images which incompletely touch on the incomprehensible? Only then, surely, would the possibility be definitively excluded of human beings like Johann Sylvanus being executed because they have difficulties with the divinity of Jesus and the Holy Spirit. Sylvanus wasn't the only martyr. I think of Michael Servetus in Geneva. I think of many others. I think especially of countless Jews.

On Wednesday 25 June 1298 450 Jews, men, women and children, were burned in Rothenburg on the Tauber. Four of them happened to be visiting Rothenburg. A survivor put up an inscription about the event. He chiselled the words:

> With a bitter soul a bitter lament . . . in memory of the martyrs of Rothenburg, who were killed and burned for the oneness of God . . .

And he ended with the confession:

> and on the third day he (God) will release us in freedom. Then my Redeemer and my Holy One will come. Amen. Amen. Amen.

This inscription brings us very near to our sermon text: God will release Israel in freedom. He will liberate those who at present suffer for the oneness of God. That is the situation of the Jews of Rothenburg. That is the situation of Moses, who was sent by the one and only God to lead Israel out of Egypt to freedom.

The credibility of any trinitarian faith depends on whether we can put it forward in the face of the suffering of Jewish and Christian martyrs for the only God, whether we recognize the God who defined himself in the burning bush as 'I AM WHO I AM' as the same God whom we worship as the trinitarian God.

How easy our forebears found that! They saw the thorn bush as a prefigurement of the crown of thorns which Jesus wore. And they saw the fire which surrounded the thorn bush as the fire of the Holy Spirit. For them, the one who said 'I AM WHO I AM' was the triune God, Father, Son and Holy Spirit.

The question is whether we can still make a convincing connection between the thorn bush and the crown of thorns. This God who defines himself as 'I AM WHO I AM' says more than that: he defines himself as a God who leads into freedom. And he doesn't just lead into an inner freedom. He leads enslaved people, slaving away with their bodies and threatened in their physical, religious and cultural existence, into freedom. Here God shows himself to be the unconditional will to liberate all men and women. And the confession of God as the incarnate Son expresses this unconditional will. God wants the whole person, even where that person is enslaved and exposed to alien powers, no matter whether this took place in slavery in Egypt, or in the torture and execution of Jesus of Nazareth, or in the slavery and torture of other people on this earth. This unconditional will for the salvation of the whole person links the God in the thorn bush to the God under the crown of thorns. Both are one.

Can we also find a link between the fire of the burning bush and the fire of the Holy Spirit? If we detached the phrase 'I AM WHO I AM' from its context, we probably wouldn't look for it in the Bible but in a modern writing – most likely in a philosophy of human subjectivity, in deep reflections on human beings and their capacity to say 'I AM WHO I AM'. And we would put it before the postmodern phase of thought – for today the end of the subject is proclaimed everywhere. That in us which says 'I AM WHO I AM' in us is claimed to be a delusion – a product of drives, physiological processes, linguistic structures. Thus we can really only say, 'SOMETHING HAPPENS. AND THIS SOMETHING SAYS "I AM WHO I AM". But this SOMETHING is wrong.' How does it come about that today we can so easily say good-bye to the certainty that we exist as inalienable persons? What is the source of this intellectual delight in abolition of the subject? One explanation is that if God doesn't say his 'I AM WHO I AM' first, human beings, God's image, fail to learn to say this I afterwards. In other words, if there is no single centre behind all the processes of the world – physical, biological and cultural development, and the whole evolution of matter from elementary particles to the cerebrum – it becomes implausible to say that there is a single centre behind all the physiological, chemical and cultural process of our life. So I think that the one who says 'I AM WHO I AM' in the burning bush has taught his image to say 'I AM WHO I AM'. He calls to men and women, 'You are destined for freedom. You are destined for more than simply functioning in dependent relationships, being a product of genes and socialization. You are destined for a responsible life.' God's call will lead you out of any captivity – often on a painful way through the wilderness – in order to confront you with yourself, with his demands on Sinai and his promise in exile. God wills to call you for all time: 'Fear not, for I have freed you; I have called you by your name. You are mine.' And only you can answer his call, freely and without compulsion. This freedom to answer is the spirit. This unconditional will for freedom links the fire in the thorn bush with the fire of the Holy Spirit. The two are the same.

If trinitarian faith means God's threefold will for the world as his creation, for human beings in Jesus of Nazareth, and for the spirit in his freedom, then we can with a good conscience reassure Jews, Muslims and the many sympathizers of Johann Sylvanus among us that this faith is not apostasy from monotheism.

But so far we have reached only the first stage of trinitarian belief, and not yet that second stage, which some years ago I didn't have time to explain to my son in the rush over breakfast. According to this, God exists in a threefold way not only in his decision for the world, human beings and spirit but also in himself, from the beginning, before he enters into any relationship with the world, human beings and our spirit. Wouldn't we do better to leave this immanent Trinity alone? Isn't everything that we say about it speculation – an invasion of the privy secrets of God, a matter for religious voyeurs, not for people who respect the mysteries of God? What could I have said to my son if I had had another couple of minutes at my disposal? And what can I say today, if I still have another few minutes left?

I think that the church fathers to whom we owe trinitarian faith wanted to say that God's will for the world, for human beings and for the spirit is on an equal footing. What we encounter in these three manifestations is of the same substance, is *homoousios*. God is a being in three distinguishable but equal roles. And this multiplicity in the one and only God was so important to them because they thought of God as intrinsically being love – as community, or more precisely as a community of equal rank. It would have been so easy for them to postulate some subordination in God. After all, the son is subordinate to the father. And the spirit comes third and last, just as the spirit always comes in last place on earth. But real love cannot tolerate any subordination, though it can tolerate difference. The thesis of the church fathers was that there is difference in God. But there is no domination in God. God is free of domination; God is an an-archist in the literal sense. God is an anarchist of love. The church, which is so often accused of having in many respects subordinated itself far too quickly to the emperor, resisted him on this point. The emperors also wanted a degree of subordination in God himself; they wanted both superiority and subordination in God. Over against this the church fathers set their conviction of the loving community of God. Over against this they set their vision of a love without domination in the heart of all being. Towards the end of my theological studies, in 1968, we were very much preoccupied with this insight: the only functioning commune of love, we said mockingly in respect of other communes, is the Trinity.

I concede that the Trinity transcends our capacity for knowledge. And at this point I am ready to learn from Feuerbach, Marx and Freud. Statements about God are always also statements about human beings and the world. What I hear in this trinitarian faith is an obligation to attribute equal status to God's unconditional Yes to the world, to human beings and to the spirit. In the midst of all things we live in community with them. If the heart of all things, the centre of reality, may be presented in sacred poetry as a loving community of equals, then our relationship to all things and people is ultimately not superiority and subordination. Through love all takes on the same value. Through love, creation with all creatures is seen on an equal footing to us. In love, each individual has an equally high value. Through love, the spirit is reconciled with what is alien to it.

This equality of the divine will in creation and matter, in all that is alive and in the human spirit, is comparable to someone meditating on a melting snowflake. It dawns on them – as it did on Albert Schweitzer – that 'That is you. The same will to life is there as is in you.'

Such convictions also give us access to the mystic religions of the East – and of course to the mystic currents in the Western religions: in Judaism, Christianity and Islam.

Of course trinitarian faith does not unite the religions, it divides them. It is a specific feature of Christianity. But this specific feature gives us more opportunities to gain access to the manifold experiences of God in all religions than if we neglect, deny or even abandon trinitarian faith.

But it must seem quite perverse to put physical and psychological pressure on other people in the name of trinitarian faith, to persecute and murder them. It is not the doctrine of the

Trinity that is perverse. Human beings are perverse in first transforming the conviction that a love without domination is the ground of all realities into dogmatic formulae and then killing others in the name of these formulae. Precisely because the people who did this sort of thing were not simply monsters – Frederick the Pious wasn't a monster, but he was under pressure from the emperor to fight heresies at home since Reformed Christians like him were themselves regarded as 'heretics' – we should judge the excesses of religious intolerance without arrogance, even if we must condemn them clearly. No age, no country, no individual has finally been preserved from this danger. Nor have we. We too can always only pray and hope that the message of the love of God which knows no domination, which is directed equally to the world, human beings and the spirit, will change our hearts and fill them with his peace.

May this peace of God, which is higher than all our understanding, keep your hearts and minds in God the Father, God the Son and God the Holy Spirit. Amen.

This sermon was prepared for the Trinity Sunday service in St Peter's Church, Heidelberg, on 25 May 1997. There is information about the anti-trinitarian trials in Heidelberg between 1570 and 1572 in F. Hepp, *Religion und Herrschaft in der Kurpfalz um 1600. Aus der Sicht der Heidelberger Kirchenrates Dr. Marcus zum Lamm (1544–1606)*, Heidelberg 1993, 55–80. Wilhelm von Scholz's anecdote about the heretic in Venice appears in L. Graf and U. Kabitz et al., *Die Blumen des Blinden*, Munich 1983, 154. The inscription in Rothenburg was found in 1914 in the Jewish cemetery there, and was then put in the museum, but in 1934 (!) it disappeared without trace. It was rediscovered in 1980, having been subsequently used as the pedestal for a symbolic eagle during the rebuilding of the town hall there. Cf. J. Rau (ed.), *Denkmal des Ewigen in der Zeit. 700 Jahre Franziskanerkirche Rothenburg ob der Tauber*, Rothenburger Sakrale Kunst no. 4, Rothenburg nd, 137. The complete inscription is: 'With a bitter soul a bitter lament, because we forgot the first persecutions. In order to commemorate them, I chiselled on a stone tablet the martyrs of Rothenburg who were killed and burned for the oneness of God in the year 58 according to the short reckoning, on 19 Tamus. And on the hill outside the city the inhabitants of the city put an end to us, old and young, by kindling a fire and killing us. On the 12th day of the fifth month of the sixth millennium my joy ceased and on the third day he will release us in freedom. Then my Redeemer and my Holy One will come. Amen. Amen. Amen.'

The Nightmare of Mobbing

And the descendants of the perpetrators

(Psalm 17)

A prayer of David

> Hear a just cause, O Lord,
> attend to my cry!
> Give ear to my prayer from lips free of deceit!
> Let my vindication come from you!
> Let your eyes see the right!
> If you try my heart,
> if you visit me by night and test me,
> you will find no wickedness in me.
> My mouth does not transgress,
> despite all that men do.
> I hold to the word of your lips.
> My steps follow the paths of your commandment,
> my feet have not slipped on your ways.
> I call upon you, for you answer me, O God;
> incline your ear to me, hear my words.
> Wondrously show your steadfast love.
> You save those who seek refuge from their adversaries at your right
>   hand.
> Keep me as the apple of the eye;
> hide me in the shadow of your wings,
> from the wicked who oppress me,
> my deadly enemies who angrily surround me.
> They have closed their hearts to pity;
> with their mouths they speak arrogantly.
> They lie in wait for me; now they surround me;
> they seek to cast me to the ground.
> They are like a lion eager to tear,
> a young lion lurking in ambush.
> Arise, O Lord! Confront the wicked!
> Cast him down to the ground,

and strike him with your sword.
Save me, O Lord, with your hand from these people,
from those who already have everything in life.
You fill their bodies with good things,
their sons will also have enough,
and leave what is left for the grandchildren.

As for me, I shall behold your face in righteousness;
when I awake, I shall be satisfied with beholding your form.

'They lie in wait for me; now they surround me; they seek to cast me to the ground.' We know this situation from imaginary fears which usually have little to do with reality. But I once experienced how for a couple of hours such a nightmare became reality.

I had been invited to a country bordering on Germany to give a lecture to a meeting of pastors and interested lay people. My wife came with me. As soon as I entered the room I felt a hostile atmosphere. I wasn't offered a chair. I got one for myself. My lecture was interrupted by disparaging comments. One member of the audience demonstratively read a book, and another kept snoring. I was aware that they were all waiting for me to make a mistake. After about ten minutes the door suddenly opened. A rifle barrel was inserted. Then someone stood in the doorway, aimed at me and shot – fortunately only with a blank. Everyone laughed. One person commented, 'How amusing.' And that among pastors, men and women. Was this a nightmare? Was it reality? Was I being humiliated here because I was a German, a member of the former occupying forces? Or as a representative of a particular theological trend? After a few soothing words I continued my lecture. But when the rifleman wanted to load his weapon again towards the end of the lecture I took a few steps towards him, removed the rifle, put it behind me on the wall and said, 'What's going on here is impossible.' Then I laboriously continued my lecture. During the meal which followed my wife was bombarded with banana skins and bones. No one protested. No one took action against the missiles. We said goodbye. Outside, my wife said, 'Now I know how the Jews must have felt during the Third Reich.'

When people experience over a long period what we had to put up with for a couple of hours, it's called mobbing. Someone is isolated for quite irrational reasons. Everyone demonstrates repudiation, the breaking-off of normal communication, physical intimidation, disinformation. All this drives the victim to despair. No matter what he or she does, they have no chance. There is mobbing in school class and at work. Here time and again what our psalm describes as 'They lie in wait for me; now they surround me; they seek to cast me to the ground' becomes reality. Anyone can become a victim, and for no reason.

This wickedness assumes quite different dimensions when it becomes a political programme, when it is directed not only against individuals but against whole groups. What happened to Jews and other groups, the gypsies and the homosexuals, in the Third Reich, was mobbing practised by the state. Everyday wickedness was organized to perfection. At that time we staged a hell on earth for millions of people: murder factories, the systematic destruction of human dignity. Only later did people gradually become aware of what had happened. And it is still incomprehensible. In the course of time one collective lie collapsed after another.

There was the first lie: 'We weren't aware of it.' One can reply to that with words from the book of Proverbs: 'Rescue those who are being taken away to death; hold back those who are stumbling to the slaughter. If you say, "Behold, we did not know this," does not he who weighs the heart perceive it?' (24.11f.). No, everyone experienced Kristallnacht. Everyone knew that violent attacks on the Jews were being organized and backed by the state. Everyone experienced Hitler's apartheid policy, the isolation of the victims, the refusal to show solidarity with them.

There was also the second lie: 'But the death camps were hidden from the public; they were set up outside Germany.' Yet calculations have been made as to how many people were involved in the administration and organization of death – from the transports and deportations to the end. The figure comes out at two million.

Then there is the third lie: 'But it was only the SS. The army didn't take part in the atrocities.' Unfortunately that wasn't the case – the army was involved in everything. It shared in the murders, it shared in the repression and it helped to organize the terror. Those who kept their integrity in the army need to be all the more aware of that.

The innocent victims who were persecuted at that time still cry out and leave behind a deep wound in our country. Did some of them also pray Psalm 17? One thing is certain: this psalm is still being prayed today, among us and in Israel. For me it's a great miracle that many Jews haven't given up their relationship to God despite the Holocaust. That they turn to the same God as we do when we pray the psalms is a sign of God's life. They turn to the God of justice and mercy. At the end of the psalm I find an astonishing statement about this God. The innocent victim who is being persecuted thinks of the sons and grandsons of the persecutors. He cries out to God:

> Save me, O Lord, with your hand from these people, from those who already have everything in life. You fill their bodies with good things, their sons will also have enough, and leave what is left for the grandchildren.

The same God of whom deliverance from the persecutors is expected cares for the sons and grandsons of the persecutors. And of course I feel that this speaks to me directly. We are the sons, we are the grandsons of the persecutors of that time. We are surprisingly rich in material goods. When Germany lay in ruins in 1945, no one could have guessed that fifty years later it would become one of the richest nations on earth. No one could have guessed that in this land there would be soon enough to eat – that gluttony, not hunger, would become the great problem. But human beings do not live by bread alone. That brings only outward satisfaction. So the suppliant makes a second request:

As for me, I shall behold your face in righteousness;
when I awake, I shall be satisfied with beholding your form.

We are not satisfied by riches, but by righteousness, which
makes us see God; by purity of heart, that purity which carries
with it the promise 'You shall see God.' If one has grown up in
a land of murderers, one longs for a pure heart. If one has
grown up in a land of perpetrators and accomplices, one longs
for justice so that one sees God in the face of one's neighbour!
If one begins to think in the land of the poets and thinkers, one
just cannot understand how it could become the land of judges
and executioners.

But what am I to say to my children? My answer is: Everything
that happened has entered into being and been inscribed in it.
No one can undo it. Before God it is an eternal present: the cries
of the victims, the despair of the tormented. But so too is every
attempt to help them: any indignation against inhumanity, any
form of resistance. God has the power to continue everything to
a good end. But God needs us for that. God transforms the
past into an appeal and a promise to us. You human beings
can organize hell for one another; but you can also leave hell
together. You can take human dignity away from one another,
but you can also see God's face in the other – in righteousness.

So let's listen to the cry of the innocent victims of persecution.
Let's hear it every day, wherever anyone is isolated and driven
to despair. Let's hear the cry of the persecuted when they have
come to us for asylum from other countries. Let's see that they
aren't sent back there, where torture and death await them.
Let's be clear that we are all too ready to turn away from them.
We're all too ready to howl with the wolves. Even sensitive
people can make mistakes. Even they can get caught up in
psychological terror against individuals. Those pastors, men
and women, who were a tribulation to me and my wife for an
evening, were certainly not people who lacked moral sensitivity.
If even among them for a short time all moral safeguards disappeared – how much more are all of us in danger? Fifty years

ago we once organized hell on earth. But does that mean that we've escaped it for ever? Doesn't the fire of hell still burn? Elie Wiesel puts it like this in a story:

A hasidic story. A traveller once lost his way in the forest. He wandered and wandered, day and night, quite alone, fearful and weary. Suddenly he saw a castle and was beside himself with joy. Then he saw that the castle was on fire, and he was very sorry. The wanderer thought that it must be an empty castle. But then he heard a voice crying out, 'Help me, help me. I'm the owner of the castle.' And the rabbi of Kotsk, who told this story, banged his fist on the table and cried out: 'The castle is in flames, the wanderer is lost, the forest is on fire, but the owner calls for help. What does all that mean? It means that there is an owner.' Applying that to us (Elie Wiesel added), I would like to reshape the story and say: 'The castle is in flames, the wanderer is lost, the forest is on fire, the whole world is on fire, and we are right in it, in the middle of the fire in the burning castle.'

In the Bible God is called a consuming fire. But the flame of his wrath can become the glow of his love. And the same thing is true of God's image: by his Spirit God can transform the fires of hell which we light into flames of love.

And may the peace of God, which surpasses all our understanding, keep our hearts and minds in Christ Jesus. Amen.

This sermon was given at the Wednesday morning service in St Peter's Church, Heidelberg on 7 June 1995. My wife and I had the macabre experience of the uncouth (private) pastors' meeting described in it in Copenhagen, shortly before Christmas 1979. The rifleman was not a theologian but a nuclear physicist. I should add that the two pastors who invited us later apologized to me and my wife for not having intervened. Moreover the event is quite untypical of Danish culture in society and the church. Our Danish colleagues and friends were as puzzled by it as we were. The hasidic story at the end is quoted from E. Wiesel, 'Die Massenvernichtung als literarische Inspiration', in J.B. Metz and E. Kogon (eds.), *Gott nach Auschwitz. Dimensionen des Massenmordes am jüdischen Volk*, Basel, Freiburg and Vienna [3]1986, 49.

The Open Heaven

And the poetry of the holy

(Psalm 85)

Lord, you were gracious to your land,
you restored the fortunes of Jacob.
You forgave the iniquity of your people;
you pardoned all their sin.
You withdrew all your wrath;
and turned from your hot anger.
Restore us again, O God of our salvation,
and put away your indignation towards us.
Will you be angry with us for ever?
Will you prolong your anger to all generations?
Will you not revive us again,
that your people may rejoice in you?
Show us your steadfast love, O Lord, and grant us your salvation.
I want to hear what God the Lord says,
he promised peace to his people and to his saints,
so that they do not engage in folly.
Surely his help is near for those who fear him,
that honour may dwell in our land;
that steadfast love and faithfulness meet;
that righteousness and peace kiss each other;.
that faithfulness grows upon earth;
and righteousness looks down from heaven;
that our Lord does what is good;
and our land yields its increase;
that righteousness goes before him,
and follows his footsteps.

When do we see the heaven open? When do we experience it in the midst of earth? If we were to ask people this question today, we might anticipate their answer. For us heaven opens when we are in love, when someone fascinates us erotically and we long to be near them – to be embraced by that aura which surrounds them, sensed only by the person who is in love. Incidentally, that's also true of a marriage. For (despite rumours to the contrary) that's an opportunity for two people to keep falling in love again – despite the everyday routine of love, despite times of alienation and despite all the rows.

Our psalm is a love poem. It speaks of God. There is alienation in love of God and there are rows. The psalm speaks of guilt and anger and of the longing to detect the nearness of God again. The climax of the psalm is a declaration of love by God. The psalmist listens to what God says. And he hears the greatest thing that a human being can hear. He hears God's promise that he is near – as near as a beloved in whose presence everything is good. Heaven and earth meet. This meeting is depicted in erotic images. Heaven and earth are a couple. Grace (from heaven) and faithfulness (from earth) find each other; righteousness (from heaven) and peace (on earth) embrace each other and kiss. Their love is fruitful. Faithfulness springs up from earth, and righteousness looks down from heaven.

Faithfulness and righteousness, grace and peace, are the children of this loving relationship. The decisive thing is that God himself is present here. Righteousness goes before him and salvation follows him.

We can best imagine such an encounter of heaven and earth in our poetic fantasy – in the mood of a beautiful summer night. The poet Eichendorff describes it like this:

It was as if heaven
had silently the kissed earth,
as if in a shower of blossoms,
earth now had to dream of heaven.

The breeze ran through the fields,
the ears of corn waved gently.
The forests quietly rustled,
so starry clear was the night.

And my soul

spread wide its wings.
Flew through the silent land,
as though it were flying home.

Where heaven and earth meet, God is near. It draws us. We
are at home there. All longing is stilled there – not just the
romantic longing of a summer night but also the longing for
light and life on a cold winter's night.

In the psalm, what conjures up the poetic image as a
romantic mood is a grandiose vision of reality. What we have
here are not just poetic moods, but the salvation of a land. We
have righteousness and peace, but it is rare for the two to meet.
For the sake of righteousness – because of a profound violation
of a sense of justice, because of experiences of injustice, insults
and discrimination – the worst wars are waged, on a large scale
and on a small scale, in politics and in everyday life. And where
peace prevails, it is often at the expense of righteousness. Therefore it is often peaceful only because many who are cheated
keep quiet in resignation and toe the line. However, salvation
comes to a land only when peace and righteousness embrace,
when one doesn't develop at the expense of the other.

But what we have here is more than politics. It is the whole
earth. The earth yields its produce only when it is treated fairly.
It goes on strike sooner or later when we plunder it heedlessly;
when instead of blessings we pile artificial fertilizer and pesti-
cides on it to extract more from it. And we do that constantly.
We're all afraid that nature will take offence at this, that one
day it will hit back because we're treating it unjustly. We are
even further removed from peace and righteousness in our relationship to nature.

But what we have here is not just politics and the environment. The psalm is about each individual. The promise of
salvation in the psalm is given in the singular. After a plural,
'*we*', we suddenly hear, '*I* want to hear what God is saying to
me . . .'. And this speaker now hears God's word. The speaker
knows that God speaks to those who turn their hearts to him.
And only individuals can do that. Each person has to do it for

himself or herself. No one else can open their heart in my place, either to others or to God. The heart is the quite individual, personal centre of our life. And God's word addresses this heart and says to each individual, 'In you, heaven and earth can begin to meet. Your heart is the place where heaven will touch earth. Therefore you are infinitely valuable. God's word is also a declaration of love to you. God wants you. God needs you so that here and now a light will dawn, here and now grace and faithfulness will meet, so that here and now righteousness and peace will embrace.'

The psalm is a 'Christmas psalm', even if it was composed long before there were Christmases. It speaks of what happens at Christmas. Heaven is opened. Peace on earth is proclaimed. Here what Eichendorff dreamed of on a fine summer night has become reality, not in a romantic mood but on a winter night. A child has been born in a cold and rough world. In him heaven and earth combine. And since then all men and women who open their heart to this child have a home. I think of this child as I repeat Eichendorff's last strophe once again:

And my soul
spread wide its wings.
Flew through the silent land,
as though it were flying home.

And may the peace of God, which surpasses all our understanding, preserve your hearts and minds in Christ Jesus. Amen.

This sermon was given at the last Wednesday service before Christmas on 20 December 1995, in St Peter's Church, Heidelberg. The poem is in J. von Eichendorff, *Werke 1, Gedichte, Versepen, Dramen, Autobiographisches*, Düsseldorf and Zurich ³1966, 285.

'Before the Mountains
Came into Being . . .'

Farewell to a great scientist

(Psalm 90.1–6)

Lord, you have been our refuge
for every generation.
Before the mountains came into being,
and the earth and the world were created,
from everlasting to everlasting you are God.
You make people die,
and say, 'Return, children of men!'
For a thousand years in your sight
are like yesterday when it is past,
and like a watch in the night
you sweep people away.
They are like a dream,
like grass which shoots up in the morning:
in the morning it blossoms and shoots;
in the evening it fades and withers.

When Wolfgang Paul sensed that death was approaching, he chose this text from Psalm 90 for this sermon. The psalm laments the transitory nature of human beings. Even if a life has been fulfilled, in the end it flies away like a dream. Even if it was full of success, in the end it is like withered grass. Even if it ends beyond the age of eighty, it seems to have been broken off. The dead man would very much have liked to have lived longer. He still had many ideas, a good deal of curiosity, much appetite for life in this last year. Beyond his death we may join him in lamenting the transitory nature of human beings.

However, the text directs our thoughts to what lies beyond all transitoriness, to what has always been, to what was before the mountains came into being and the earth and the world were created, or, as the literal translation runs, before the earth was in travail, giving birth to the mountains. The earth is imagined as a mother who brings forth everything. And behind it appears yet more: the whole system of reality which has brought us forth, which preserves us for a while, imposes harsh limits upon us, and to which we return. And in all this and beyond all this and behind all this, God – from eternity to eternity.

Wolfgang Paul came from a family which included many pastors. Psalm 90 is a piece of his Protestant tradition. But this psalm has also spoken to physicists, time and again. For example, Georg Lichtenberg could compose pointed aphorisms critical of religion and at the same time confess that he had never been able to read this psalm 'without an exalted, indescribable feeling'. What he felt here was more than anything that we could discover by science about those most elementary process of nature which were already taking place before the mountains came into being. This is no additional knowledge on top of all our physical knowledge, but a call which can come to us in the midst of all our knowledge, if we open ourselves to the one who is from eternity to eternity. It is a voice which cries out, 'Return, children of men.' It calls to us who are alive, 'Entrust yourselves again to life. Return to the life which has been shattered by the death of a person!' And it calls to the dead man, 'Return to that which was from eternity to eternity, to the hands of God.'

Wolfgang Paul has returned to a silence which escapes our understanding. Conversations with him are at an end. Often they have been broken off. Nevertheless they continue in us, in all those who were close to him. It is almost indiscreet to want to get involved in them. Yet it is my task to introduce into these conversations with ourselves the voice of the one to whom the psalm bears witness.

The voice does not persuade us to think it good that human beings have to perish. On the contrary, it rebels against this. The psalm says that it must be the wrath of God that we have to perish. It appeals against this anger at the goodness of God. It appeals to something that is not devalued by transitoriness. At the end it mentions where it finds this goodness and kindness of God despite all transitoriness. We read: 'May the favour of the Lord our God be upon us, and establish the work of our hands upon us.'

So that is the point of the psalm. Transitory though human beings are, their action can succeed. They may be only a tiny moment in that one day which embraces a thousand years, but they can investigate more than a thousand years. They may only be a phenomenon on the surface of a small planet, but they can calculate the universe. They may be deeply rooted in biological evolution, but they are the first free creatures, who can limit the fight over the distribution of opportunities in life. They are perhaps an insignificant offshoot of the universe, but they can make contact with the one who has created the universe. Transitory though they may be, that is where their dignity lies. In this they can detect the kindness of God, the graciousness of being, and for that they can be grateful.

It is precisely this to which we are called today: to be grateful for a life which has come to an end. We have reason to be grateful. A blessing lay upon what Wolfgang Paul did – as a researcher, as a teacher, as a scientific organizer and as a human being.

A blessing lay on what Wolfgang Paul did as a researcher. He has extended our knowledge of nature. He kept having new ideas for experiments. He was imaginative in thinking about what could be done differently. And even if initially he came up against scepticism, he followed up his ideas with determination. A truth became visible in his life which is an obligation to us all. We are created to create, to be creative. There are many possibilities of this in life – from the garden to the kitchen, from building to making music. But the experimental physicist is to be envied: he can be creative in the medium of the most elementary processes. He can be a small co-creator with the great creator: any experiment leads beyond nature, beyond what happens anyway. The very terminology reveals this surplus, as in talk of cages or traps for ions. Here something is done which would never take place without human intervention. And yet it simply serves to bring out what has always taken place and is always taking place. It is as though human beings could reconstruct the thoughts of God at creation by themselves being creative.

Therefore transitory though human beings may be – like grass which shoots up in the morning and withers in the evening – a blessing lies on their action: they, the creatures, may become co-creators in the knowledge of nature. They are the image of God.

A blessing lay on what Wolfgang Paul did as a teacher. He encouraged a creative climate of which he was the centre. He shared his ideas. Younger people could experience research at first hand. Many of those present will be able to testify to this better than I can, since I know it only at second hand. But it is important for me to emphasize it here. In science, too, there is a kind of treaty between the generations: with increasing age the older scientists increasingly work to ensure that the younger scientists will be able to work. And if in doing this they succeed in bringing about a creative climate without the emotional smog of disputes over prestige and blocks in communication, they really are a blessing.

Therefore here, too, transitory though human beings may be – like grass which shoots up in the morning and withers in the evening – a blessing lies on their action if as teachers they win over and inspire the next generation for science.

A blessing lay on what Wolfgang Paul did as a scientific organizer. Much of what he has set up will survive his death. It needn't be enumerated here; it is well known. I would stress just one thing: in recent years he invested a good deal of time and energy in encouraging the international exchange of knowledge and research – not only in physics but in all disciplines. At a time when the divisions between cultures and nations are reviving again in an uncanny way, it is vitally important for the scientific community to remain international and to go on the offensive in emphasizing its international character. We have only this one earth. It is entrusted to us together. We will not cope with this task unless together we keep developing new scientific imagination all over this earth. That includes an international culture of knowledge and research. Granted, this is given with science. But human beings have the freedom to deny it and betray it.

So here too, however transitory human beings may be – like grass which shoots up in the morning and withers in the evening – a blessing lies upon them when they come together beyond the frontiers of cultures and nations.

However, at this hour of farewell the most important thing to do is to give thanks for our fellow human being Wolfgang Paul. His humanity showed itself at the very point where death invaded life. He lost his father at the age of fifteen, so after leaving school he first trained as a mechanic, in order to give financial support to his mother and five brothers and sisters. Later he had a happy marriage of thirty-six years, which was also a foundation for the difficult wartime and post-war years with all their crises. When his first wife died after a long, severe illness, he had supported her with loving care. And after her death the memory of their long years together filled him with gratitude. His second marriage was also happy. It was in a time of great success, but was also under the shadow of advanced age, illness and death. And precisely for that reason it took on depth and intensity.

So once again: transitory though human beings may be – like grass which shoots up in the morning and withers in the evening – a blessing lies upon them when they are bound up in love with their fellow human beings.

It is not my task to sketch a complete picture of this life which has come to an end. All the pictures that we paint of another person are only fragments. All the pictures that we paint of ourselves are only fragments. We cannot even fathom ourselves. God alone knows the true nature of a person. And when we perish, all that remains of us for eternity is what we are in the judgment of God.

The dead man had a biblical text put above one of the doors of the great lecture room in the Institute of Physics in Wegelerstrasse. It comes from the Letter of James: 'But be doers of the word, and not hearers only, deceiving yourselves.' That suits an experimental physicist who got down to work and for whom there was no difference between mechanical physicists and others. It suits the teacher who didn't want to train just consumers of knowledge, but physicists who would engage in independent research. It suits the scientific organizer, who took it for granted that science serves life – and not death and destruction. That is why he subscribed to the Göttingen Declaration. And it fits the person Wolfgang Paul. He had integrity, and his actions matched his words. Finally, it suits the Letter of James, which here outlines its picture of a whole existence: when we are in harmony with God, we are also in harmony with ourselves.

God, the Lord of life and death, has recalled Wolfgang Paul. A rich life has come to an end. Though his life a voice speaks to us all today: 'Be not only hearers of the word, but doers, not deceiving yourselves.'

We would be deceiving ourselves if we suppressed our transitoriness, if we were unwilling to perceive that we have only a limited time; that we will die. Therefore Psalm 90 prays, 'Lord, teach us to remember that we must die, so that we may become shrewd – so that we may have a wise heart.'

But who is so shrewd? Who is so wise? Shrewdness and wisdom do not mean a Stoic imperturbability. On the contrary, at this hour of farewell we may mourn openly. It is a good thing not to fight against that. But let us also be deeply grateful at the same time. An old piece of biblical wisdom is that blessing can be hidden in suffering if we open ourselves to suffering and at the same time activate everything in us that makes gratitude possible. Christians learn this by looking at the figure of Jesus:

when the blows of life hit us and the ground shakes under us, our courage to live will constantly be crucified and buried. But there is the promise that it will rise to new life – through the power of the one who created being out of nothingness.

Through the goodness of the one who was before the mountains came into being and the earth and the world were made.

Through the grace of the one who will be when the mountains no longer exist, and who calls us, both the living and the dead.

The mountains will give way and the hills fall,
but my grace shall not depart from you,
and the covenant of my peace shall not fail,
says God, your Redeemer.

And may the peace of God which surpasses all our understanding keep our hearts in Jesus Christ. Amen.

This sermon was given at a funeral service for the physicist Wolfgang Paul on 13 December 1993 in the Schlosskirche in Bonn. Wolfgang Paul (10 August 1913 – 7 December 1993) had been a professor in the University of Bonn since 1952 and since 1979 President of the Alexander von Humboldt Foundation, which promotes international exchanges among scientists. In 1989 he was awarded the Nobel Prize for Physics for his pioneering contributions to the physics of elementary particles. He was one of the signatories to the Göttingen Manifesto of 1957 in which leading nuclear scientists spoke out against the arming the German Federal Republic with nuclear weapons. The quotation from G.C. Lichtenberg appears in a self-portrait by Lichtenberg in the *Südelbüchern*, B, no. 81. In full, it runs: 'As a boy he already thought very freely about religion, but never sought credit for being a free spirit. However, he does not believe everything without exception. He can pray ardently, and has never been able to read Psalm 90 without an exalted, indescribable, feeling. For him "Before the mountains were brought forth . . ." is infinitely more than "Sing, immortal soul . . ." He does not know which he hates more, young officers or young preachers; he could not live long with either of them.' In G.S. Lichtenberg, *Aphorismen, Schriften, Briefe*, Munich nd, 30.

Poems as Signs of Life

Mourning for a life between sickness and poetry

(Psalm 139)

Lord, you have searched me and known me.
You know when I sit down and when I rise up;
you discern my thoughts from afar.
You search out my path and my lying down,
and are acquainted with all my ways.
Even before a word is on my tongue,
Lord, you know it already.
You surround me on all sides,
and hold your hand over me.
This knowledge is too wonderful for me,
and too high; I cannot grasp it.

Whither shall I go from your Spirit,
and whither shall I flee from your presence?
If I ascend to heaven, you are there;
if I lie down with the dead you are there too.
If I took the wings of the morning
and dwelt in the uttermost parts of the sea,
even there your hand would lead me,
and your right hand would hold me.
If I said, 'Let darkness cover me,
and the light about me be night,'
even darkness would not be dark to you,
the night would be as bright as the day.
Darkness is like light with you.

For you have made my inward parts,
you formed me in my mother's womb.
I praise you,
because I am wonderfully made.
Marvellous are your works;
my soul knows that well.

My frame was not hidden from you,
when I was being made in secret,
when I was being formed below.
Your eyes saw me when I was not yet formed,
and all days were written in your book,
which were to be and none of which yet was.

How precious your thoughts are for me, God!
How vast is the sum of them!
If I were to count them, they would be more than the sand.
In the end, I am still with you.

Search me, God, and know my heart!
Try me and know my thoughts!
And see if I am on a wicked way,
and lead me in the way everlasting!

We have all been expecting the death of Inge Vielhauer for a long time. Now that it has taken place and she has gone away into a silence that we do not understand, there is a gap. All conversations with her are finally over. Probably many people are thinking, as I am, 'Did we say to her everything that we should have said? Did we show her enough how much we love and treasure her?'

I share your grief in this hour of parting. But when Inge Vielhauer asked me to speak to you today, she gave me a task which points beyond such sorrow, the task of comforting you. I am to comfort you with something which has permeated her whole life: a great gratitude. Gratitude towards God, who gave her this life and has taken it to himself; gratitude towards those people who supported her through this life; gratitude today in particular to the people who were around her in the hospice until she died. Gratitude to the sisters, relatives and helpers; gratitude to the visitors old and young; gratitude for all the care, friendship and help. Gratitude to all those who made her aware that this life is a precious life – to the last hour.

I am sure that many of us also feel grateful to her – particularly for this last year. She herself has helped us to prepare for parting from her. She has helped us by speaking openly of her impending death. She has helped us to come to terms with our uncertainty about sickness and death. For some of us she was a help towards preparing inwardly for our own illness and death.

For this time she chose a psalm which expresses her gratitude to God and life. This psalm was for long a companion to her in life. She would be glad if today we could feel linked to her beyond death when we reflect on it. Its theme is God's presence in living and in dying.

Lord, you have searched me and known me.
You know when I sit down and when I rise up;
you discern my thoughts from afar.
You search out my path and my lying down,
and are acquainted with all my ways.

Whither shall I go from your Spirit,
and whither shall I flee from your presence?
If I ascend to heaven, you are there;
if I lie down with the dead you are there too.
If I took the wings of the morning
and dwelt in the uttermost parts of the sea,
even there your hand would lead me,
and your right hand would hold me.

The psalm is a fine piece of poetry. Inge Vielhauer's life was to end with a poem. That is no coincidence. For her whole life was a life with and in poems.

I know that some people laughed about her love of poems. Many people had no inkling of how much inner strength she derived from them. In her youth she often had to spend a long time lying in bed because of her illness. During this time she built up an inner world with the help of poems that she had learned by heart. This was a world of fantasy, feeling and beauty to counter the monotony of a life on mattresses. That is how she kept alive within. That is how she survived a long illness without psychological damage. For her, poems became signs of life – pointers to a successful life.

People didn't always understand. The pastor who confirmed her drew her attention to the tension between the world of the beautiful and the Christian faith: isn't Christian faith about the overcoming of pain, suffering and guilt? Isn't it also about what isn't beautiful? Don't the most beautiful poems pale when death is near?

These questions concerned Inge Vielhauer very much as a young adult until one day, walking along the banks of the Neckar, she became certain that the two are not mutually exclusive. Thereupon she resolved not to be led astray by the tension between the beautiful world of poetry and the darkness of this world, so familiar to Christian faith. Both are part of God's creation. God is everywhere. Poems can open our eyes to this. A modern poet put it like this. Her name is Silja Walter and she is a nun.

> The kingdom and the glory
> are also in
> anemones and nettles,
> Lord, for the one
> who sees it,
> who sees through everything –
>
> There is also a song of praise in us,
> of praise and thanksgiving,
> silence and
> amazement at you,
> for the one who sees it,
> who sees through everything –
>
> In us too there is parable
> and truth
> and life and festivity –
> a glimmer and a sketch of the fair Creator
> and Lord,
> here among us.
> His fragrance fills all

the world,
and behind everything
his face shines,
for the one who sees it,
who sees through everything
with seeing eyes.

Inge Vielhauer had the kind of eyes which could see the
Creator through the world. But she had to keep forsaking this
beautiful world, because it was invaded by the world of pain,
injustice and suffering.

In the Nazi period she experienced how Jewish friends had to
emigrate. She experienced the expulsion from school of teachers
whose politics was mistrusted. She experienced spying, when
she joined a group around the Catholic student chaplain.

Later she married a man marked by the war: for a while he
was handicapped by a severe head injury, but nevertheless,
despite many illnesses, he achieved great things. However, he
was often completely absorbed in them, which she didn't find
easy.

She devoted herself to foreigners who learned German from
her. She helped them to cope with everyday problems. And she
was horrified at the wave of xenophobia which has broken out
among us in recent years.

Wasn't this real world a contradiction to the world of the
beautiful? She could have given three answers to this: one with
modern poems, a second with the Bible, and a third with an old
Irish blessing.

The first answer is that poems are open to the world of pain.
Modern poems in particular do not want just to depict the
beautiful, but to complain about the ugly. They seek to be a
protest. They know that their world of beauty is bound up with
the world of suffering. One of the poets whom she most
treasured, Hugo von Hofmannsthal, put it like this:

But some must die down there
where the heavy rudders of the ships ply;
others live up above at the tiller,
know the flight of birds and the lands of the stars.
Yet a shadow falls from that life
over the other life,
and the light is bound to the heavy,
as to air and earth.

Her own suffering and that of others kept casting a shadow over Inge Vielhauer's life. But she opened herself to it. She wanted to be open to it, as modern poems are open to this un-beautiful world, just as they bring us down to those who die below, in the lower levels of life, where it is dark and sad.

The second answer appears in the Bible. It is comparable to the first. For without suspecting it, many modern poets take the same ways as God in the Bible, indeed in our psalm. In it God does not remain up there – somewhere in heaven, where there is no suffering, no pain, no death, where there are no tears. First of all this psalm, too, takes us to heaven. It says:

Whither shall I go from your Spirit,
and whither shall I flee from your presence?
If I ascend to heaven, you are there.

But the continuation is decisive: God is not only right up there but also right down below, in the lower levels of life, where it is dark and sad. Then we find:

If I lie down with the dead you are there too.

Now Inge Vielhauer has her resting place among the dead. She has gone before us on the way to the land of death. We do not know this land. We often find it uncanny. But the psalm says that whatever awaits us there, God himself is there. He is not only in the light but also in the darkness. He is not only in this life but also in death. We are always in God's hand, and nothing can tear us from it.

> If I ascend to heaven, you are there;
> if I lie down with the dead you are there too.
> If I took the wings of the morning
> and dwelt in the uttermost parts of the sea,
> even there your hand would lead me,
> and your right hand would hold me.

If Inge Vielhauer were to meet today her old pastor who drew her attention to the tension between the world of the beautiful and Christian faith, she could tell him, 'This tension has been overcome. God himself is beauty, but he wills to be present in the world of death, suffering and pain. And the modern poets also want to be open to this world; they want to be provoked and hurt by it.'

And if the old pastor were to ask, 'How can you be so certain?', she would have yet a third answer. It would take the form of an old Irish blessing. This blessing does not speak directly of God's presence but of Christ's presence. If God is present in Jesus, in a human being who withstood the fear of death, who was tortured and crucified, then God is really present with us – even when death comes. Then he is near to us and does not forsake us, even if we think that we are being forsaken. The deceased had this blessing beside her during her last months. It goes:

> Christ be with me, Christ within me,
> Christ behind me, Christ before me,
> Christ beside me, Christ to win me,
> Christ to comfort and restore me,
> Christ beneath me, Christ above me,
> Christ in quiet, Christ in danger,
> Christ in hearts of all that love me,
> Christ in mouth of friend and stranger.

And, I would add, in life and death.

Inge Vielhauer endured her long illness in this confidence that God was also present with her in suffering. Now she is with God. God is caring for her. We no longer need to care for her. *We* no longer need to ask whether she has everything that can make life easier for someone in the last days of her life, so that this life remains human life to the last hour – as valuable as all life. We no longer need ask whether she will withstand the days of her illness without inner collapse. She has completed her course. She rests in peace.

If we are anxious, it is for ourselves and the living. We should ask ourselves, 'Will we experience God in living and in dying? Will we use the days when we are healthy and strong for ourselves and our neighbours in such a way that at the end we say, "Thanks, that was good"? Will we suffer inner collapse if a lengthy illness grinds us down?' Will we have the strength of Inge Vielhauer, who until shortly before her death would smile at anyone who came to visit her, so that I often left the sickroom less disturbed than when I had entered it. To the last she lived in such a way that one really felt another old Irish blessing: 'May you greet whomever you may meet . . . with a friendly smile.'

Inge Vielhauer wanted me to give you a comfort which only God himself can give, which one only senses if one opens one's heart to God and makes contact with him. I know that God has become distant for many people. They have no contact with him. Yet God calls. We overhear his voice. He also calls to us through this life and this death, 'Turn back to me.' He has made a covenant for life with each one of us. He holds us fast. He leads us through happy and dark hours. He remains with us in living and dying. He assures us:

> The mountains will give way and the hills fall, but my grace shall not depart from you, and the covenant of my peace shall not fail, says God, your Redeemer.

And may the peace of God which surpasses all our understanding keep our hearts and minds in Christ Jesus. Amen.

Poems as Signs of Life

This sermon was given on 28 October 1993 in the chapel of St Joseph's Hospital, Heidelberg at a funeral service for Inge Vielhauer (12 June 1920 to 24 October 1993). Inge Vielhauer had very bad health at the beginning of her life, between the ages of four and sixteen. In the long periods of illness she built up a rich inner world – to combat the monotony of lying and resting – learning poetry by heart. She studied German, the Romance languages and English, and made her own scholarly contributions above all in mediaeval studies. Between 1954 and 1977 she was married to the New Testament scholar Philipp Vielhauer. She spent the end of her life in the hospice attached to St Joseph's Hospital. Poems were also her companions in her long stay there. The poem 'Flowers' by the Benedictine Silga Walter, in *Beim Fest des Christus. Messe – Meditationen*, with a commentary by E. Hofmann, Zurich 1975, 84f., is also an expression of thanks to the nuns who ran the hospice and filled it with a life-affirming atmosphere even in the face of death. Inge Vielhauer lived there very much longer than she had expected to. The poem 'But some must die down there . . . ' appears in Hugo von Hofmannsthal, *Sämtliche Werke I, Gedichte 1*, ed. E. Weber, Frankfurt am Main 1984, 54.

Signs of Life from God

The testimony of Israel in the face of the Holocaust

(Isaiah 44.6–8)

Thus says the Lord, the King of Israel and his Redeemer, the Lord of hosts: 'I am the first and I am the last, besides me there is no God. Who is like me? Let him proclaim, let him declare and set it forth before me. Who has announced from of old things to come? Let them tell us what is yet to be. Fear not, nor be afraid; have I not told you from of old and declared it? And you are my witnesses! Is there a God besides me? There is no Rock; I know not any.'

Today is Israel Day. Today many Christians are reflecting on the significance of Israel. For me, everything that can be said about that is bracketed between two pieces of data.

The first is one of the first mentions of Israel in history, on the victory stele of Pharaoh Merneptah in the thirteenth century BCE. Here this Pharaoh boasts that he has destroyed Israel's future. Israel no longer has descendants. Israel enters world history with an account of its annihilation.

The second is again the account of an annihilation: the Holocaust, the annihilation of six million Jews, among them one million children, organized like a factory process, planned in our country and carried out by Germans. Fifty years after the end of the Holocaust one is as uncomprehending as at the beginning – looking upon it with grief, shame and anger, yet knowing that no grief, shame or anger can ever do justice to this event.

And precisely for that reason Israel and Judaism have finally become a criterion for humanity. At a very early stage I learned from my teachers that the touchstone of humanity is how one relates to Judaism and antisemitism. But for us Christians Israel is even more. Since 1945 Christian theologians – at first hesitantly, and then with increasing intensity – have attempted to redefine and formulate this 'more'. I am attempting to do so by choosing a text from Isaiah 44, a text which once redefined the role of Israel in the world, then too after a great catastrophe, the destruction of the first temple at the time of the exile.

> Thus says the Lord,
> the King of Israel and his Redeemer,
> the Lord of hosts:
> 'I am the first and I am the last,
> besides me there is no God . . .
> And you are my witnesses!
> Is there a God besides me?
> There is no Rock;
> I know not any.'

Here the significance of Israel is clearly defined: Israel is a witness to the one and only God. Israel is the monotheistic conscience of the world. That is its task towards humankind. Therefore it is the 'mediator of the covenant' for the human race, as the prophet says. I could now go on to say a good deal about that – in postmodern times, when all monotheism has fallen into disrepute for being dictatorial. Many of our contemporaries are engaged in bidding farewell to the one God and seeking freedom by recognizing a multiplicity of ultimate values – formerly these would have been called gods. There is a search for freedom which involves a renunciation of a single view of life; a search for freedom which involves denying that life has an inner centre; a search for freedom as patchwork identity.

However, I would prefer to put what is important for me in the monotheistic faith of Israel more positively. This one God defines himself in his first commandment as a God who leads to freedom: 'I am the Lord your God who brought you out of the land of Egypt, out of the house of bondage. You shall have no other gods before me.' Who are these other gods? Why are they rejected? Why are they denied? Why this suppression of plurality which is so offensive to the postmodern mentality? These other gods are different from the God of Israel; they do not lead out of the house of slavery but into dependent relationships. By defining himself as the one who leads to freedom, the God of Israel defines any God who does not lead to freedom as an idol. The Christian God also becomes such an idol if he does not lead to freedom.

He did not lead to freedom when Protestantism became National Protestantism, and understood itself as the religion of the Holy Protestant Reich of the German Nation, in which Catholics and Socialists were felt to be disruptive alien elements and were fought against.

He does not lead to freedom when the Catholic hierarchy, with reference to him, rejects communion with the Protestant churches and threatens to stifle the unrest which has arisen among Catholics with authoritarian reflexes.

He does not lead to freedom when fundamentalists – in Christianity, Judaism and Islam – attempt to impose their convictions in politics and faith with psychological and physical violence.

When one reflects on God in an abstract way, one can soon leave out the notion of freedom. But when one speaks of the God of Israel, of that God who leads his people out of the house of slavery in Egypt, then freedom becomes the decisive criterion for distinguishing between God and idols.

Yet more can be said: the criterion is not just what God does but what the human beings who appeal to him do. God imposes an obligation on them to lead into freedom those who are not free. This task, too, is given to Israel in Second Isaiah:

> . . . I have made you a mediator of the covenant for the
> human race,
> a light of the nations,
> to open eyes that are blind,
> to bring out the prisoners from the dungeon,
> from the prison those that sit in darkness (Isa. 42.6f.).

Because it contains such great texts, I love the Old Testament. I am attached to the God of the Old Testament and respect the people that feels a commitment to such statements. And I can well understand all those among us who would like to belong to this people – not as children of Abraham through birth, but through faith.

How fine it would be if we could now say, 'Don't Christians and Jews have the same God? The same ethic of freedom? Can't we easily tolerate what separates us? Couldn't we agree that for Jews freedom is given through the Torah but for Christians through Christ?'

However, with such well-meaning statements the difficulties begin. I am thinking on the one hand of the difficulties that we Christians cause for Jews, and on the other hand of the difficulties that Jews inevitably cause for us. It wouldn't be a good thing to leave such difficulties aside. They have to be discussed, particularly on Israel Day.

The difficulties which Christians cause for Jews have their basis in the New Testament. There too there is talk of that God who leads out of slavery into freedom. But in Paul this slavery also includes the Torah – that law which according to Jewish understanding first gives freedom. According to Paul, the freedom that Christ gives is freedom from the law. Certainly we must add that according to Paul Christ wants to free not only *from* the law as a letter which kills but also *for* the law as a spirit that brings life – that law which is fulfilled in the commandment to love. But precisely for this reason he criticizes the law. First, because it contains a series of ritual commandments which in his view unnecessarily separate people, above all circumcision and food laws. And secondly, because all commandments – even the most sublime ethical commandments – can be misused to devalue others and put pressure on them. Here Paul is speaking on the basis of his own experience. Before his conversion he was a Jewish fundamentalist. Appealing to the law, he had pressurized and persecuted a deviant minority, the Christians. He was liberated from this fundamentalist attachment to the Torah in a painful but liberating experience. For him Christ took the place of the Torah. What causes difficulties for us today is that he always tended to identify his former fundamentalist Judaism with Judaism generally.

Nevertheless, his critical questions to the Torah remain. Suppose that one day the Temple Mount in Jerusalem again came into Jewish hands – wouldn't even many Jews have hesitations about implementing the cultic commandments of the Torah in a literal, i.e. a fundamentalist, sense? That would mean a resumption of the bloody sacrificial cult, killing animals every day for the greater glory of God. Wouldn't Paul's distinction between the letter in the Torah that kills and the spirit that gives life arise in such a situation? I'm certain that if the problem does arise, the Jewish rabbis will hit on a humane solution (as they always do).

Nevertheless, it isn't unfair to put such questions. What is unfair is to draw a conclusion that has long been drawn from the New Testament criticism of the law: it has been thought that it is no longer necessary to listen to Israel's testimony to the one and only God. Israel is thought to have been superseded in religious questions. For Christians, it no longer exists as a factor which is important for faith. But the statement 'You are my witnesses' also applies to the present, and in a special way.

That brings me to the perplexities that the Jews cause for us. If Christians have critical questions for Jews about their understanding of the Torah, Jews have critical questions for Christians about their faith in Christ – the conviction that with him the Messiah has come, that in him redemption has begun, and that an authentic relationship to the Father can be mediated only through him: 'No one comes to the Father but by me.'

How can one say that the Messiah has already come if the world is so unredeemed? Aren't people making hell for one another – today in Bosnia, yesterday in Cambodia, fifty years ago in Auschwitz? And even if one were to grant that redemption begins with an inner transformation in human beings, that it is only a drop of eternity which falls into the transitoriness of life, what has this inner transformation of Christians already achieved? Could the Holocaust have happened if even just a relevant number of Christians had been inwardly transformed?

Certainly we must never forget that those who planned the Holocaust did so out of a decidedly anti-Christian ideology. After the final victory the churches were to be forced into line and Christianity was to be abolished. But these people could plan and carry out their crime only because in our culture a Christian anti-Judaism paralysed people's consciousnesses. It paralysed their consciences when they should have cried out – at that time, when Jews were discriminated against and deprived of their rights in a way which was plain to all, through the race laws and Kristallnacht. Where was inner redemption to be detected in the hearts of Christians here? Where was the belief in the God who leads from slavery into freedom? Is it redemption if a drop of eternity falls into the human heart – and a drop of the poison of antisemitism enters the heart with it?

These questions must cause us deep perplexity. They are justified. One can react to them only with a readiness to repent. Christianity shares in the guilt for the Holocaust. Many Christians have precisely the same view as I do.

But precisely in this situation Israel becomes God's witness to us. If we listen to the voices of Jews grappling with the Holocaust, we soon notice that here there is a dialogue with the same God in whom we too believe. Let's listen to some of these voices.

A rabbi says: The Holocaust was a catastrophe like the destruction of Jerusalem and the temple. It took place because of our sins. So let us repent. Let us draw power from the catastrophe to change our lives.

Another protests: No, it didn't take place for *our* sins. Here was an accumulation of the transgressions of *others*. Israel endured the wickedness of all. It endured it vicariously for *all* that *all* might repent.

A third finds this notion intolerable: In that case you're making the murderers God's instruments. No, the catastrophe cannot be interpreted – any more than the death of a single innocent child. The incomprehensibility of the violent and cruel death of millions is no greater riddle than that of an individual. For every death is the death of an individual. A world history dies in each person.

A fourth rabbi objects: You forget that here a whole people is being dealt with. We must learn to become independent and adult as a people. In the covenant with God we must become senior partners instead of junior partners. God has left us alone so that we could adopt a new role towards him.

A fifth says bitterly: If God allowed all this, his covenant with his people is broken. In that case we are alone, and God is absent. It is night – and we can only wait until day returns.

A last insists: We may not wait. Absolute evil is at work among us. It threatens us. There is only one answer. We must resist evil. Jews and others should never again be defenceless victims. We must work towards that.

Today the rabbis of Israel are also formulating vicariously for us a faith which can resist absolute evil. Who could be a more credible witness to this faith than Israel? Israel was not God's witness in the world only in Isaiah's time. It also is today. That is how the conservative Jewish theologian Elias Berkovits sees it. Here is what he says:

> Why is anyone chosen? Why has God created human beings? Why has he created anything at all? No one can know that. But we do know one thing. No other people on earth could have borne what we have borne, and nevertheless have remained faithful to God's calling to admonish and warn humankind.

Aren't we all directed to this voice of Israel? I hear it particularly clearly in a little story which is set in the last war.

At that time many rabbis met in Vilna and discussed who was to blame for the Holocaust. Was it human beings? And if so which? Was it God? After a long discussion they voted in the middle of the night. And they arrived at the verdict that God was to blame. And they condemned him. There was a long silence. No one spoke. It was pitch dark. After some time, however, the sun rose. A rabbi opened the window and said, 'Morning is here. It is time for morning prayer. Let us praise God.'

This story bears witness to an authentic experience of God – even without Christ. But in depth this experience is also akin to belief in Christ. Christians, too, know the night of the darkness of God. Time and again our faith, too, our affirmation of God and life, is crucified and buried. And we too experience the miracle of the resurrection of our faith from nothingness, together with the resurrection of Christ. Who could deny hearing the voice of God in the living Judaism of today?

But let's leave aside these basic theological problems, which perhaps we shall never be able to answer completely satisfactorily, as is the case with the various experiences of God in different religions. I'm now thinking of quite existential problems.

If during your life you sink into long phases of a darkness of God, if you condemn and curse life and God, then you should stick to such experiences. Wait with the rabbis in Vilna for the morning when it is again possible to praise God. Look at the crucified and risen Christ with whom your courage to live is crucified and recreated from nothing.

It is the same God who occurs in both places as an enigma and as a miracle, as dark night and the light of morning. It is the God who defines himself as the God who leads into freedom: in the Old Testament from the house of slavery in Egypt and Pharaoh Merneptah's war of annihilation; in the New Testament from sin, fundamentalist fanaticism and death. And so too today: from the darkness of God to the morning in which a spark of the eternal morning light falls into your heart – just a drop of eternity, perhaps only a drop in a sea of tears and misery, but a drop of eternity which can transform everything.

Sometimes you will have to wait a long time for the night to pass away. But if things are really bad for you, think of the rabbis in Vilna. Every morning is an opportunity to begin to praise God again and to feel grateful for life.

Think of Jesus Christ! Every morning is an Easter event in which life 'rises' again and walks upright, as you are called to do as the image of God.

This waiting doesn't justify any suffering. It doesn't legitimate any misery. It doesn't reinterpret any darkness as light. It simply says:

There is life – incomprehensible, wonderful life that is given and fulfilled – despite absolute evil, despite the darkness of suffering and guilt and futility.

Jews and Christians today are united in this experience, and not just today. I have chosen two hymns from our legacy of tradition for today. Both come from the sixteenth century. Here we find similar experiences.

First of all a hymn of praise. It praises God that we too have been chosen, together with Israel; that we can share in Israel's task and Israel's experiences.

Then a lament from Luther. He sees the true nature of Israel in this waiting for the morning: an example for all Christians. The somewhat patriarchal words really come to life for me when I think of the rabbis of Vilna.

Whether it takes until the night
and on to the morning,
my heart will praise God's might,
and neither doubt not fear.
So assume Israel's true nature
which was begotten of the spirit
and waits for its God.

And may the peace of God which surpasses all our understanding keep our hearts and minds in Christ Jesus. Amen.

This sermon was given on 20 August 1995 in St Peter's Church, Heidelberg. The Jewish voices on the Holocaust are a free rendering of A.H. Friedlander, *Das Ende der Nacht. Jüdische und christliche Denker nach dem Holocaust*, Gütersloh 1995. The quotation from the Jewish theologian Eliezer Berkovits comes from his *Faith after Holocaust*, New

York 1973, and is quoted from Friedlander. The story of the rabbis in Vilna is a free rendering of H. Zahrnt, *Mutmassungen über Gott. Die theologische Summe meines Lebens*, Munich and Zurich 1994, 125. The two hymns mentioned at the end of the sermon are Sartorius's 'Praise God the Lord, all you nations', and the fourth stanza of Luther's 'In deepest need I cry to thee'.

The World as Absurd Theatre

Suffering as a school of resistance

(Isaiah 50.4–9)

The Lord God has given me the tongue of a disciple, that I may know to how to revive the weary with a word. Morning by morning he wakens, he wakens my ear to hear as a disciple. The Lord God opened my ear, and I was not rebellious, I did not turn backwards. I gave my back to those who struck me, and my cheeks to those who pulled out my beard; I did not hide my face from shame and spitting. For the Lord God helps me; therefore I have not been confounded; therefore I set my face like a flint, and I knew that I should not be put to shame . . . He who vindicates me is near. Who will contend with me? Let us stand up together. Who is my adversary? Let him approach me. Behold, the Lord God helps me; who will declare me guilty? Behold, all of them will wear out like a garment; the moths will eat them up.

The text of this sermon is one of a series of texts which speak of an enigmatic figure, a prophet and martyr. In this text he himself speaks.

We will understand his words better if we imagine ourselves in exile: banished and separated from what is holy to us, separated from our homeland in which we were so happy, separated from life and separated from God. For this text was once addressed to the Israelites in exile. They had been exiled to Babylon, separated from what was holy to them, the temple. The Babylonians had destroyed it. They were separated from their homeland, which had been devastated by war. And many people thought that they had also been separated and banished even from God.

At that time many people were saying, 'We have been defeated by the Babylonians, and our God has been displaced by Marduk, the Babylonian God. So let us follow the stronger gods, the values and gods of the victors.' The prophet directs *his* message against that. It is the message of the one and only God, the message that the Babylonian gods do not exist, that they have not defeated the God of Israel. Rather, this one and only God has brought about this defeat and exile. Disaster and salvation come from him alone. Even the end of the exile lies in his hands. With this message the prophet was the first to advocate a consistent monotheism in Israel. Something new began with it.

But the prophet had little success. He was pleading a hopeless cause. Today we can indeed recognize in him the beginning of a new faith to which the future belonged. But his contemporaries saw him only as the representative of a faith which was dying out. They hardly listened to him.

So his disciples adopted a different course when they brought together his words. Not only his words were to disseminate his message, but also scenes from his life and death, which deliberately remain shrouded in mystery. They knew that the mysterious is attractive and the uncanny attracts attention. So we find that as part of the book of Isaiah they put together the script of an enigmatic play. Its title is 'Waiting for Adonai', and its subtitle 'Absurd Theatre in Three Scenes'.

The first scene is a school class. There is a teacher and there are many pupils, including a model pupil. Instruction takes place every morning, since the morning lesson is when people are freshest. The teacher is an advocate of the educational system of the ancient Near East. The method consists of saying something, having it repeated and then learned by heart. If it isn't got right, it's helped along with a slap. Anyone who doesn't chastize his pupils doesn't love them. The model pupil is all ears every morning. He learns everything: the whole history of Israel, the creation, that God himself has said, 'Behold, all is good.' He learns the Sinai story, the Ten Commandments, the laws of righteousness and the demands of mercy. He learns everything and soaks it all up. He isn't rebellious.

The second scene is set in the street. There is a rough house involving skinheads. They set on the model pupil. It is not clear whether they are schoolmates or strangers. Be this as it may, they heap on the pupil the blows that his teacher spared him. Model pupils don't make themselves popular. The one who is set upon reacts in a paradoxical way. He doesn't defend himself. He willingly turns his back. He is struck on one cheek and offers the other. They pluck out his facial hair and say, 'You're not a man.' He allows it. They spit on him and say, 'You're filth.' But he stands there as though all this were nothing to do with him. His face turns to stone. It is as though he were putting an invisible wall between himself and the humiliations.

The third scene is judgment before the gate. The tormented pupil makes a complaint to the judges. He calls out to his opponents, 'Come on, let's have a lawsuit.' But no one arrives. He cries out on the empty stage, 'Come on. Don't be afraid.' But no one appears. He calls out, 'Aren't you coming? Your punishment will catch up with you anyway. You'll fall to pieces like a moth-eaten garment.' But no opponent emerges. No one owns up to having fallen upon the defenceless person. His cry echoes in a void.

That was already *avant-garde* art in the Near East, a provocation. Of course there was the standard reaction. 'The Adonai Theatre ought to be closed. We have other problems. At least it's worth playing the good old shows, e.g. David and Goliath, where the righteous person is rewarded and the villain punished. But what about this piece without an exalted moral, in which the righteous suffers and things go badly with him? Where nothing makes sense? We already have enough brutality in reality, we don't want to see it again in the theatre.' Moreover there was already a great theatre in Babylon, the Marduk Theatre. Why not put on a couple of guest performances there? The plays put on there were much more optimistic, much more contemporary. And one heard that the Babylonians were very happy with their theatre. But there are also supporters of the Adonai Theatre.

The first says: the play must be taken literally. Don't we teach our children the ethical and religious traditions of our people, and doesn't that make them suffer even more? Why? Because life goes by different rules from our morality. We teach them, 'Love your neighbour as yourself. Love even your enemies as yourself. Help your enemy when he is in need.' But reality is different. There the law of the strongest applies. We find no love of neighbour and mercy there. The most sensitive of our children risk collapsing under the pressure. So let's be realistic. Let's change our educational system. Let's say that our religious and ethical traditions aren't programmes for success. Everyone else thinks that anything that doesn't bring success is worthless. But we say, 'What brings you a beating in life can be the truth.' We say, 'Even when you suffer, you haven't necessarily done anything wrong. On the contrary, the righteous have to suffer.' In this way we achieve at least one thing: our children suffering under the evil of the world say, 'Outwardly things may be going badly with us, but this distress needn't gnaw away inside us. Others may spit on us, but that doesn't mean that we have to spit on ourselves. Others may beat us, but that doesn't mean that we have to lay into ourselves as if we were the failures, we were the guilty, we were worthless. Let's cry out. The judge is on our side and on the side of our children. So let's keep putting on the play, because it restores to us the dignity that others want to take from us.'

The second defender of the play argues for a metaphorical inter-pretation. In the drama, representatives appear: an image for the subject-matter, an event for the life, an individual for the group. The pupils in the play represent the prophets. The prophet stages his life in such a way that his message makes us reflect. To this end he demonstratively assumes the role of a pupil who suffers innocently. In this way he unsettles those of us who reject his message and maltreat him. 'Look,' he says, 'You're laying into an innocent. You're rejecting me although I'm defending the truth.' He's putting our norms and con-victions in question. He's shaking our self-confidence more than someone who emerges as a victor. Modern sociologists would say that he's choosing the strategy of self-stigmatization, the demonstrative adoption of roles which social morality despises, in order to compromise the existing system of values and norms.

The third defender of the play proposes a collective interpretation: the fate of the whole people is depicted in the fate of the pupil. Israel is God's model pupil. Israel is the only one among the peoples who took his teaching seriously. Israel is the first people to penetrate to the knowledge of the one and only God. In so doing it deviated from its environment. It became an outsider. Some admired it, but the enmity and hatred were even greater. Throughout its history it was assailed and persecuted. Its temple was destroyed; its synagogues were burned down. And yet it addresses an appeal to all, a double appeal: to acknowledge God and to hear God's hidden message in the sufferer, that God is on the side of those who suffer and are put to shame. This message is still a scandal for all those who glorify power and strength, a scandal for leaders and rulers. But at the same time once and for all it has become a criterion for humanity, for the way in which people behave towards the weak and inferior. Our attitude to Israel and the Jews has become a criterion for humanity.

A fourth defender of the play insists that drama is ambivalent. Any interpretation opens up the way for others. The pupil in the play is a representative of the prophets, the prophet is a representative of Israel, and in the last resort Israel is a representative of humanity. This comprehensive interpretation, too, is indicated in the work. For Israel is to make God's covenant with his creatures accessible to all. We are all to recognize that we have left the animal kingdom only when we overcome the law of the strong – when the more adapted, the fitter, the stronger do not simply establish themselves, but use their strength to protect the weak, the suffering and the broken. Only where we recognize true life in the weaker and in the sufferers have we escaped our evolutionary prehistory. Only then have we made the transition from animals to human beings. Only then do we become the image of God.

Dear people, no one has yet been able to clarify the ambiguity of our text. Poetic works are open texts with many interpretations. Indeed they are texts with pre-interpretations, a foretaste of something that has never yet happened. Therefore Christians could read this text as a forecast of the fate of Jesus. This Christian understanding of the text is legitimate in so far as all other interpretations are in harmony with it.

The first interpretation: Jesus is the son of Israel. Jesus is the pupil who has adopted for himself Israel's great traditions of God's mercy and love of neighbour. He embodies them in such a convincing way that they become accessible to all, even Gentiles.

The second interpretation: Jesus is the prophet who demonstratively adopts despised outsider roles. He teaches people to offer the right cheek when they are struck on the left. In this way he shatters the unbroken aggression, interrupts the spiral of violence.

The third interpretation: Jesus is the Jew who is executed by Gentiles. His fate is the fate of Israel, as Marc Chagall has painted it. In the city, pogroms are raging against the Jews. The synagogue is burning. But the Crucified has the Torah scroll in his hand and is again maltreated in his brothers and sisters.

And the last interpretation: Jesus is the new person, the beginning of a new humanity in which the law of the stronger is overcome, in which life no longer lives at the expense of other life. In him this new life becomes symbolically visible in the midst of the old world. This old world is God's poetry, God's creation. In terms of poetry it is absurd theatre. But in this work of God Jesus appears vicariously for all human beings. And therefore this absurd theatre has a meaning after all – especially if you assume your role in it; if you also take part in for others vicariously, in the spirit of Jesus; if you too are ready to offer your back.

Beyond doubt, the play which we perform is often sorry and absurd. We're experiencing that again today. The social chill in our society is increasing. Educated people define humane criteria for dealing with aliens but refuse to live anywhere near asylum-seekers. In a painful debate it is suggested that the old and painful are an unwanted economic burden. Antisemitism is trivialized. What are we to make of highly legalistic verdicts which do not recognize the contempt for the victims in the denial of mass murders? In this way false signals are given. And dismayingly, again a synagogue is on fire in our land. Don't we notice how at all levels of society we can abandon criteria which were still taken completely for granted yesterday – criteria for dealing with those on the margin, who are different, who attract prejudice and aggression? Bit by bit we are losing some of our humanity.

Yet we shouldn't complain, 'Why is this world so absurd? Why are people so inhuman? Why doesn't God do something about so much absurdity?' God already has done something against it. God has already done something tremendous. God has created you. God has created you to oppose it, and not to howl with the wolves. God has created the many people who protested against the corruption in our society in candlelight processions. God created the people who gathered yesterday in front of the synagogue in Heidelberg as a protest against the burning of the synagogue in Lübeck.

Next year will be decisive for the development of our country. It will be decisive whether in the many elections the parties which represent the spirit of inhumanity receive a rebuff. Each of us has some responsibility here. We can all make it clear to those around us that abstention only helps the extremists. The more people stay at home, the easier it is for them to get over the five-per-cent hurdle.

So let's oppose the change in social climate in our country. It isn't a natural event. It's the consequence of a long-term pollution of the moral environment. Boundaries have been crossed in nationalism and antisemitism. Even among the educated and the intellectuals the mood is: 'Times have changed. The humane measures of yesterday need to be adapted to rougher times. Everything is too social, too humane, too liberal. Now leading opinion is rightly adopting new values and gods.'

In this situation, listen to the words of the prophet in exile. The word of God which obliges us to be humane still applies. The word of the one who led Israel out of the house of slavery still applies. His words are still true:

> I am the first and I am the last
> and beside me there is no God.
> Who is like me?
> Let him come forth and cry,
> let him announce it and present it to me.
> You are my witnesses.
> Is there a God but me?
> Is there a rock?
> I know of none.

In the theatre of his world, God has assigned Israel the role of his witness. He has summoned us as witnesses through Jesus. Let's remain true to our calling – even if times are taking a different direction, even if the world seems to us to be an exile. And let us pray God to give us courage and power not to fail him again, when we have to bear witness for him and for Israel.

This sermon was given on 27 March 1994 in St Peter's Church, Heidelberg. The synagogue in Lübeck had been set on fire on 25 March. There were several apartments in the synagogues, and the perpetrator(s) took into account that those in them might die. The fire was put out in time. That same week – shortly before the arson attack – the Federal Court of Justice decreed that the denial of the Nazi mass murders was not in itself a criminal offence; this was only the case when there was evidence that this denial was the consequence of a racist attitude. The reference to educated people who define humane criteria but refuse to live near asylum-seekers had a topical background in Heidelberg at that time: when a hostel for such people was to be built in an area almost exclusively populated by well-to-do members of the university, petitions were collected against it. Even a Nobel prize-winner signed, but later withdrew his signature.

Signs of Life for the Church

Protestantism between the Feast of the Reformation and Thoughts on Kristallnacht

(Isaiah 62.6–7, 10–12)

Upon your walls, Jerusalem, I have set watchmen; all day and all night they shall never be silent. You who are to remember the Lord, take no rest, and give him no rest until he establishes Jerusalem and makes it a praise in the earth . . . Go through, go through the gates, prepare the way for the people; build up, build up the highway, clear it of stones. Set up a sign for the peoples. Behold, the Lord has proclaimed to the end of the earth: Say to the daughter of Zion, 'See, your salvation is coming; look, his reward is with him, and his recompense before him.' And they shall be called 'The holy people', 'The Redeemed of the Lord', and you shall be called 'Sought Out', 'A City No Longer Forsaken'.

My involvement with the text of this sermon began with a mistake. I was uncertain why it had been proposed for this Sunday. Its theme is Israel and Jerusalem. It speaks of the hope that Jerusalem will shine out in new radiance despite catastrophe and exile. I asked myself: was the text chosen with a view to Kristallnacht, which we shall be thinking about next week, on 9 November? Was it meant to be a text to counter the humiliations and the maltreatment to which Jews among us were exposed fifty years ago? I couldn't have guessed how topical it would become today. For like me, shortly before the service so many of us have heard of the murder of the Israeli Prime Minister Yitzhak Rabin – another setback on the way to a restoration of Israel. To that extent the sermon texts fits today. But why did some Protestant liturgical commission at one point choose this text without being able to envisage today's situation? Now Isaiah 62 is the text for Reformation Day, which was last week. In the tradition of Christian interpretation Jerusalem is an image of the church. The theme was not to be the restoration of Israel, but the restoration of the church in the Reformation.

I read the text through once again. Does it fit the Reformation? My first impression was that it's too triumphalistic, a song of praise for the entry of the redeemed. The committee which chose this text for Reformation Day was probably thinking of a solemn Protestant open-air service with anti-Catholic outbursts. But I had to correct this impression. Reading it through once again, I was struck by the fact that the committee has omitted some verses – and chosen only two sections of text. I have to concede that these omissions fascinate me more than the chosen texts. So I shall begin with them.

The first omission, in the middle of the text, is a promise that Jerusalem will never again be conquered by enemies:

> The Lord has sworn by his right hand and by his mighty arm:
> 'I will not again give your grain to be food for your enemies,
> and foreigners shall not drink the wine for which you have
> laboured; but those who garner it shall eat it and praise the
> Lord, and those who gather it shall drink it in the courts of
> my sanctuary.'

Puritans were probably involved in the liturgical commission which omitted these verses. For them there was to be no talk of eating and drinking on Reformation Day. But I guess that it wasn't ascetic tendencies which caused the omission, but the talk of strangers and enemies. That doesn't fit love of enemies. It doesn't fit Protestantism. For all the diagnoses agree that Protestantism has lost its hostile stereotypes. Some people think that's its problem. In my youth, even before one had an inkling of what Protestantism meant, it meant not being Catholic. To sum up the prejudices of my youth, two things were understood by Catholicism: on the one hand authoritarian dictatorship by pastoral letters and the confessional, and on the other hand the seduction of the people by the spiritual sensuality of the mass and the less spiritual sensuality of carnival. Catholicism meant living in unfreedom. The pope decides; the morality of the church holds. Communities have to toe the line. Such hostile stereotypes are harmless compared with those of Luther. For him it didn't mean something unreal, 'If the world were full of devils . . . ' For him the devil was very real – and at work in the papacy, Catholicism and, to our dismay (in Luther as an old man), also in the Jews. What Luther wrote about the Jews before his death reads like an incitement to Kristallnacht. In the face of such hostile stereotypes and diabolic imagery, isn't it reassuring that Protestantism has lost its hostile stereotypes? That it deletes references to enemies from its sermon texts so that crazy preachers somewhere don't get the idea of expounding them?

Or have we given up our hostile stereotypes too early? At the centre of Catholicism today aren't we experiencing a revolt against what for some is the last surviving system with totalitarian tendencies in Central Europe? The referendum is meant to introduce democracy into the church, to get Catholicism out of the dead end into which it has been directed by encyclicals on sexual morality and the priestly office. In this situation should we reactivate our hostile stereotypes and once again sing, 'If the world were full of devils' – understanding the Catholics as devils? But wouldn't that be absurd? After all, we can see that Catholics are different. They're having a referendum. Many of them are seized by the spirit of the Reformation. Many are more Protestant than we are! How should we deal with this new situation?

With the doctrine of justification the Reformation has given us a precious legacy that can help us. It says that God's will is to acknowledge human beings unconditionally – even when he cannot acknowledge their actions. God distinguishes between person and work. Let's apply that to our problem. Let's accept Catholics unreservedly, but not accept everything that some do and think, even more so if they have the majority in Conferences of Bishops. We don't need any enemies, but we need clear and objective demarcations so that the rebel Catholics don't put us to shame. We must be allowed to say openly (even if it is probably not the view of everyone in this church): what official Catholicism says about birth control is in my view irresponsible. And I would add: the inner freedom with which most Catholics put themselves above this is in my view exemplary. We must be allowed to say openly: the exclusion of women from the priestly ministry is sexism. We must be allowed to state clearly that the dogma of the infallibility of the pope is arrogance. We must be allowed to assert plainly: the claim to be the one true church, regarding all the others as lost sheep, is itself one of the greatest errors that sheep can get lost in. If we want to keep the Catholics who really exist as friends, we must reject some Catholic positions which exist just as really. That is what I mean when I say, 'Let's accept the persons but reject some positions. Let's make a distinction between person and work, between individual and opinion, between Christians and the church system.'

But this distinction is also helpful in another way. Let's look at our own works and actions. Anyone who calls for the equal rights of women in church ministry with a Protestant solemnity should be aware that it was only in the 1970s that women were given equal preaching rights with men in most Protestant churches. The last state church yielded only in 1991. Academic theology didn't make much of a contribution. A theologian of the past generation whom I admire as a person of integrity still noted in 1960 that a Christian woman 'cannot more thoroughly mistake and deny the dignity accruing to her as a woman than if in marriage and the church she wishes to attain the position held by the man'. He goes on to say that 'the whole of the Christian message is at stake' in this question. Here we can really only say that we are all sinners, Protestants and Catholics. The fact that we ceased from some sin a few years earlier doesn't justify anti-Catholic hostile stereotypes, quite apart from the fact that sins continue to be committed in this field. Some women have the impression that the academic institutions in particular still have some opportunities to make up for old sins or to desist from some sins in the future.

Now for the second omission in our text. I ask myself why our Protestant liturgical commission omitted a marvellous declaration of love at the beginning of the text. The prophet makes it to Zion in God's name:

> You shall be a crown of beauty in the hand of the Lord, and a royal diadem in the hand of your God. You shall no more be termed 'Forsaken', and your land shall no more be termed 'Desolate'; but you shall be called 'My Delight', and your land 'Beloved Wife': for the Lord delights in you, and your land has a loving husband. For as a young man marries a virgin, so shall your architect free you, and as a bridegroom rejoices over the bride, so shall your God rejoice over you.

We are first struck by the eating and drinking – and then also by the pleasure of this love. How good such a declaration of love would be for Protestantism today! It would do Protestants good to be assured: 'God delights in you. You aren't a wall-flower or a Cinderella, but God's beloved, God's friend, God's consort and God's wife!'

Perhaps we Protestants could then take more delight in our church. Here we can learn from our Catholic fellow-Christians. Incomprehensible though it often is, they still love their church. They love it like a mother who has grown old and eccentric. And they keep forgiving it.

When we Protestants make mistakes, we can often hardly forgive ourselves. Perhaps church leaders in the Democratic Republic made mistakes when they repudiated anti-Communist reflexes (which I still think to be right). But that doesn't mean that one can declare left-wing Protestantism to be the great enemy of the church, instead of seeking the enemy where it really was, in the secret police apparatus.

Perhaps we Protestants made mistakes when we reacted to the challenge of modernity with ever new demythologizations. One piece of theological iconoclasm followed another. But that doesn't mean that all this intellectual creativity can be described as the symptoms of an over-cerebral Protestantism. On the contrary, I see the problem as being that Protestantism at present is so remarkably silent over the reinterpretation of its faith. We need a good deal of brainwork still.

Perhaps we Protestants had some illusions when we wanted to build a church on the basic notion of freedom. Many people, too many people, have understood this freedom as freedom to turn their backs on the church. But does that mean that we should stop being a confession of freedom? Should we give up the great experiment of a church which more than any other religious community leaves its members the freedom to decide where and how they shall identify themselves, commit themselves, communicate?

Because this Protestantism has lost its attraction, nowadays it often seems 'forsaken': not like a bride whom one woos, not like a young girl in whom God delights, but like someone paralysed by frustration. A cultivated depression permeates the Protestant temperament. And precisely for that reason I say that in the message of justification we have an anti-depressive means of great power, a sign of life from God, a sign of life for the church. Why? Let me explain.

Sorrow is part of life, including the life of a church. But depressions only arise when we consolidate them through disparaging comments about ourselves. If we say 'I'm a failure' and not 'That was a mistake'; if we say 'I'm no use' and not 'That was too much for me'. If we say 'My life is a wilderness' and not 'I have to go through this wilderness'. It is such generalizations that turn unavoidable sorrow into depression. My concern is that Protestantism talks itself into collective depressions. And we must guard ourselves against precisely that by the conviction that God justifies the person, even when he repudiates that person's actions. God distinguishes between person and work, human being and destiny, identity and success. God doesn't evaluate the failure of works as the failure of the person. God says, 'You are good although not everything that you do is good.' God says, 'I recognize in you my image, although you do much to damage that image.' God says, 'You are loved, although the harshness of life often gives the impression that life

87

doesn't wish you well.' Today as a church, too, we hear this message: 'Do you think that you're forsaken by God? No, God loves the abandoned. God delights in you. God delights in all men and women who put themselves at his disposal.'

So far I've preached only on the verses that have been left out. Finally, a few words about the sections of text which have been selected. They too contain an important message.

The first section says that the prophet has set watchmen on the walls of Jerusalem (in the name of God). The security system is to warn against enemies. But these watchmen have a remarkable function. They are never to rest, but to keep on making a noise and thus remind God at last to bring about his salvation. They are to be a burden on God, to give him no rest. Exegetes argue whether the watchmen stand for guardian angels in heaven or prophets and believers on earth. At all events, the selection of this passage is primally Protestant. Protestantism is an alarm system – one, moreover, which I am convinced sometimes gets on God's nerves. We Protestants are fond of sounding an alarm on earth – and do so with the conviction that in this role we are as important as the most senior archangels in heaven. Our problem is that sometimes our alarm system doesn't function. In Kristallnacht – or better, in the period beforehand – it remained silent despite individual warning voices. Here the sirens should have howled. And our anxiety today is that perhaps we are again sleeping through situations where we should have given the alarm. On the other hand, such 'alarmism' is exhausting. I have to keep asking many young Protestant men and women not to live in a constant state of inner alarm. It's possible to ask so much of the conscience that it achieves nothing – except loss of sleep. What if it makes people ill, if it leaves behind severe psychosomatic traces? That's the problem. And yet this somewhat exhausting Protestantism is my home. I love it with all its faults. Its motto is a maxim of Fillip de Marnix, the sixteenth-century Dutch Reformer: *'repos ailleurs'* – rest is elsewhere. Here there is unrest and activity. Here there is moral pain. Here there is a state of alarm. Rest is elsewhere. But where? Where do we find this rest?

Protestant unrest can make one ill if one doesn't compensate for it. And our liturgical commission also seems to have had an inkling of that. For the second section of text which it has selected illustrates a second basic maxim of Protestantism which was formulated in Saxony. It runs: 'A safe stronghold is our God.' Rest is only in God. God is the rock of eternity. God is the fortress of being. Some Protestants see themselves as zealous watchmen on the walls of God's citadel, to prevent certain people from getting in: no gays and lesbians, say some; no Catholics, say others; no Jews and Muslims, says a third group. But the text sketches a different picture of the city of God. In this city the gates are wide open. The watchword is 'Go through, go through the gates! Clear the way for those who stream in! Be open to all those whom God brings in!' But who are they? Let's recall that originally this text doesn't speak of the church; it speaks of Jerusalem, of Israel. It wasn't a mistake when I first understood it in this way. And if one reflects on it for a long time, it contains a deeper truth. Protestantism will not find rest without being open to Judaism. The fact that Reformation Day and 9 November, the date of Kristallnacht, are so close together should make us think. Without a new reform of Christian faith in which it loses its anti-Jewish elements and corrects some other things, but also enriches itself with some things, we will no longer be able to celebrate the past Reformation with a good conscience. Judaism is our mother religion. No one can be at peace with himself without being at peace with his mother. And indeed that applies to the whole world: there can be no stable peace in the world without peace with Israel.

I'm aware that such openness is too much for many people. But we aren't alone in this dream of the opening up of the city of God. Centuries after the Old Testament prophet in Isaiah 62 had dreamed of the scattered and exiled Jews streaming into the city of God, another Jewish prophet took up his dream. He had a vision of people from all nations streaming into the city of

God, into God's kingdom. Gentiles would come from every direction to recline at one table with Jews. We hear nothing of a conversion of the Gentiles. The food laws which separate Gentiles and Jews no longer play a role. This Jewish prophet, Jesus, is at the same time the foundation of Christianity. He could develop this vision because he was convinced that God is ready to accept all people – regardless of their actions, their culture, their origin and their gender. He didn't teach justification in the words which are familiar to us Protestants from Paul, but he lived it. And in this way he opened up the gates to the nearness of God. He opened them wide – wider than we think possible.

This message of justification is the safe stronghold within Protestantism. It gives the rest of eternity in all the unrest of the heart. It assures us that how much we do isn't the issue. And precisely because of that, it gives us freedom to yield to the unrest of the heart and to be restlessly active. This message of justification is the dawning splendour of eternity in the midst of life. It assures us that it doesn't matter whether we're successful or not. For the picture that God has of us doesn't depend on our success. It isn't put in question by our failures. And precisely for that reason, we can resist success and failure. Precisely for that reason, our unrest remains. Through it more life comes to life. But rest is elsewhere. Rest is in God. However, it is God's will for his spirit to dwell in us so that nothing can deprive us of courage to live and to die, and his peace fills us in all the unrest between cradle and grave. May this peace of God which surpasses all our understanding keep your hearts and minds in Christ Jesus. Amen.

This sermon was given on 5 November 1995 in St Peter's Church, Heidelberg. Traditionally there is a reference to the Reformation in this church on the Sunday after Reformation Day. The Israeli Prime Minister Yitzhaq Rabin had been murdered on 4 November. Referendums took place in the Catholic churches of Austria, Germany and Switzerland in 1995. The most important points were: 1. Development of a church of brothers and sisters; 2. Full and equal rights for women; 3. A free choice between celibate and non-celibate forms of life;

4. A positive evaluation of sexuality as an important part of the human person created and affirmed by God; 5. Good news instead of threats (cf. *Wir sind Kirche. Die Kirchenvolksbegehren in der Diskussion*, Freiburg 1995, 13f.). The statement of the Protestant theologian on the question of the status of the woman in marriage and the church is by P. Brunner, 'Das Hirtenamt und die Frau', *LR* 9, 1959/60, 298–329: 322. Fillips de Marnix (1540–1598) among other things studied theology in Geneva with Calvin; he translated the psalms and served William of Orange as a politician. C.W. Mönnich, *Bürger, Ketzer, Aussenseiter. Die Geschichte des Protestantismus in ihren Grundzügen*, Munich 1984, 8, characterizes the feeling about life among Reformed and Lutherans as follows. 'The Lutheran knows that "God's word and Luther's teaching" will never ever pass away. That radiates certainty. It puts the son of Luther at a considerable distance from less assimilated confessions. He does not need to have the last feeling that is addressed in Marnix's remark about St Aldegonde, *repos ailleurs*: rest is elsewhere, not here. From his safe stronghold he can look on seekers from afar.'

Making Reality a Parable

And God's new righteousness

(Matthew 20.1–16)

For the kingdom of heaven is like a householder who went out early in the morning to hire labourers for his vineyard. After agreeing with the labourers for a denarius a day, he sent them into his vineyard. And going out about the third hour he saw others standing idle in the market place; and to them he said, 'You go into the vineyard too, and whatever is right I will give you.' So they went. Going out again about the sixth hour and the ninth hour, he did the same. And about the eleventh hour he went out and found others standing; and he said to them, 'Why do you stand here idle all day?' They said to him, 'Because no one has hired us.' He said to them, 'You go into the vineyard too.' And when evening came, the owner of the vineyard said to his steward, 'Call the labourers and pay them their wages, beginning with the last, up to the first.' And when those hired about the eleventh hour came, each of them received a denarius. Now when the first came, they thought they would receive more; but each of them also received a denarius. And on receiving it they grumbled at the householder, saying, 'These last worked only one hour, and you have made them equal to us who have borne the burden of the day and the scorching heat.' But he replied to one of them, 'Friend, I am doing you no wrong; did you not agree with me for a denarius? Take what belongs to you, and go; I choose to give to this last as I give to you. Am I not allowed to do what I choose with what belongs to me? Or do you begrudge my generosity?' So the last will be first, and the first last.

Sometimes outsiders draw attention to treasures that we have without knowing it. That's what happened to me with this parable. I learned to see it in quite a new light when I made the acquaintance of a Japanese Buddhist who became a Christian because of it. He learned Greek (the original language of the New Testament) in order to be able to understand it better and

92

came to Europe so as to be able to study theology there for a couple of semesters – and all because of Matthew 20.1–16.

What fascinated him so much about this text? He told me that there is a basic problem in life, uncertainty as to whether one's own life has any value. Without being asked, we raise the question, 'Are we worth more than others? Are the others worth more? Have they more potential, more competence, more charm, more success?' Such comparisons increase our uncertainty. For any judgment is relative, and can be put in question. The Buddhist thought that there were only two consistent answers to this problem: Buddha's answer and that of Jesus in Matthew 20.

The Buddhist answer runs: the question 'What am I worth?' is based on an illusory presupposition – that there is such a thing as an 'I', a self. All existence is suffering. Everything brings grief, and all suffering is ultimately grounded in the fact that we regard our self as something real, instead of a chance crossing of causal chains. Fundamentally everything is equally valueless. Once one has learned that, then all uncertainty as to the value of one's own life disappears. For this life is an illusion. And of course the quest for a 'value' of life is also an illusion. Those who free themselves from this quest, free themselves from their selves, gain a deep inner peace.

But Jesus' answer in Matthew 20 is just as consistent. All human beings are of equal value, despite the fact that they are often extremely different in their actions and fortunes. Whether you've done much or little in life, whether your life is long or short, whether it's full of success or failure, whether you're happy in your relationships or suffer in them – regardless of this, all human life is of equal value. And it is in no way illusion, but reality. This disappearing and suffering self – in a world in which everything is in some kind of pain and everything is suffering – is the most real thing in the world. It's valuable. Thus through Jesus and his parables we could attain to a certainty which is similar to the great inner tranquillity of the Buddhist. For it comes to the same thing whether we say that everything is unconditionally valueless – and so don't need to worry at missing something – or say 'Your life is uncon-ditionally valuable', so you can be certain about the decisive thing in life, even if you don't have much that others have. The Buddhist became a Christian because in the end he couldn't and wouldn't regard his own personal life as an illusion.

I found this former Buddhist very sympathetic, above all because even as a Christian he attached some truth to his Buddhism. In addition, this Japanese showed me that we can retell the parables of Jesus best today as parables about col-leagues at work, conflicts over work and remarkable employers; as parables about pupils and teachers. And time and again in these rewritten parables, he showed (in the style and in the spirit of Jesus) that all uncertainty about the value of our own lives melts away when we are confronted by Jesus with an unconditional value, God.

When I was reflecting and meditating on this parable – and was looking for an idea for this Bible study – I suddenly saw the figures in it before me in my mind's eye. It was as though they were running over my desk. They were engaged in vigorous dis-cussion. At first I could hardly understand them. Such parable people lead a wafer-thin life in our imagination and are very sensitive. Something on my desk disturbed them. So I moved the many exegetical books and commentaries to give them more room. And in fact now I could understand them. I listened to them with fascination. They seemed to have an inkling that they were only parable people – notions of their creator. And they also had an inkling that outside their world of parables there is another, real world (our world) with real people (like us). Above all the steward, who in the parable, too, stands between the owner and the workers, showed this. It seemed to me that he was a steward not only of vineyards but also of parables. Let me tell you what I heard in my inner excursion into this world of parables.

The day about which Matthew 20 reports is over; work is done and pay has been handed out. The grumblers are going home. Their criticism of the owner of the vineyard hasn't yet died down. In self-justification, one of the grumblers says, 'First we're being cheated of our just recompense and then morality is being twisted – as though we were the wicked ones because we insisted on fair recompense for our work. If our landowner really had a social conscience, he would have employed all the workers at the same time in the morning, and made them all begin together. That would have had three advantages:

First, all the work would have been done by the ninth hour.

Secondly, all would have deservedly received the same recompense.

Thirdly, all could have gone home earlier and had a longer evening to celebrate.'

The steward points out: 'Just think, we're only a parable. Imagine a parable which went like this: A landowner had a good deal of work. He employed all the workers, paid them all equally, and all went home content. Wouldn't that be a boring story? Would anyone be interested in it? People who really exist must recognize their real problems in us, otherwise there will be no contact with them. Only then will we parable people fulfil our task of formulating and communicating a message to them.'

In my imagination I listened to a second parable person intervening. He defended the landowner. When he employed ten people at the beginning of the day he thought that he could do all the work with them. But he had miscalculated. Why? The first workers weren't much use. So he had to employ new ones. But they, too, fell short of his expectations. Only the last ones saved the day's harvest. So despite the short period of time that they worked, they were worth very much more than the first. The last were the most efficient. Moreover, the recompense takes into account not only the time worked, but supply and demand. In the evening the supply of workers was scarce, and the urgency of the work was great. So objectively the workers employed last were worth more. That's how it is now on the labour market.

But here the steward of the parable protests. 'You're confusing the real world and the world of parables. In the real world things are as you say. Money expresses a person's worth.

Some people have a great deal of capital. If they sleep eight hours, during this period they will have earned as much interest as others earn in a whole year. Since they earn a great deal with little time and effort, by objective criteria their achievement is very great. These are the high performers in the real world. And then there are others in the real world who have four jobs in one day: 1. half a day's work at the office; 2. education: supervising school work and teaching life-style and manners; 3. housework: cooking, washing, ironing, organizing, thinking – above all thinking about everything; 4, care: care of an old mother. But they don't earn much. A lot of work and little pay, so according to the logic of the real world they aren't performers. And then when they're worn out people tell them, "You aren't what you used to be," and dismiss them. That's what happens in the real world. But surely you don't want to introduce this immorality into our parable world? We parable people too have our honour. We should hold up a mirror to people who really exist so that they are shocked at their immorality, but we shouldn't help them to make light of it.'

Finally, a third worker in the parable speaks. He says: 'Basically, the owner kept all his promises. He made a firm contract for a denarius only with the first workers. Already to the second group he simply promised fair recompense. He left open how much that was. He made no promises at all to the third, fourth and fifth groups. So the first had two advantages: first, right at the beginning of the day they didn't have to worry whether they would be taking anything home at the end. They had a day without anxiety. And secondly, they knew precisely what they would be getting. They could plan. But all the others lived in a state of uncertainty as to whether they would find work at all. And when they had found work, they worked without knowing what wages they would receive. So the first were doubly privileged. It just isn't fair if they in particular feel disadvantaged at the end – they were better off than all the others.'

Here the steward of the parables can agree: 'I believe that you're right. We've been invented by our creator to make it clear that the real question is not whether the landowner is just but whether we are just, and whether it is just for us to become envious of one another. The question is one of *our* justice. Can we bear being treated equally?'

Then a fourth parable person speaks, as though he had suddenly had a bright idea. 'I've got it,' he says. 'Our creator wanted to test us. He wanted to test us to discover whether we can rejoice that all the workers get what they need. But we didn't pass the test: we grumbled. We wanted the last to be worse off than the rest. So he tells us, "I got you right. You're an envious people with no solidarity. You don't want everyone to get a minimum wage – regardless of performance, but in keeping with his or her needs. You're not ready for a higher justice. But that's my ideal: to give everyone a different wage, depending on the time they've been working and their performance. Then everyone goes home and voluntarily shares things out, so that the first automatically give to the last and they have enough to live without needing to beg. That's what I wanted. But I guessed rightly, You aren't ready for it. You don't bother to create equality among yourselves. So I have to do it for you. I have to show you how to deal with your possessions. You have the freedom to distribute them equally, as I do. And now you're protesting against my justice! This protest rebounds on you: if only your sense of justice towards one another were a little greater, I could leave the distribution to you. But your eye is evil: you look enviously at one another. Especially those who have more than others, the first among you, have a crazy need for others to be worse off than they are. Otherwise, they say, what's the point of efficiency and high performance? And where would we be then?'

The steward agrees: the protest against the owner's justice is a protest against our inability to achieve fair distribution for ourselves.

But other parable people reject this interpretation outright. They exclaim: 'You've always taught us that we parable people are only ideas who point to their creator. We exist only because we are transparent to him. But now you're telling us that the issue is our relationship with one another. It's not our relationship to our creator, but interpersonal justice. You interpret our parable existence like some real people do. Among them there are socialist, liberation-theology and humanist interpretations of the kind that you're putting forward. But in the real world they're put forward only at church conferences. So please don't infect our beautiful parable world with that kind of thing.'

Our parable steward is hard pressed. He defends himself. 'Look at other stories from our parable world. They too are about interpersonal relations.

There are two about a judge, but the point isn't that one gets justice from the court and the other doesn't. The point is that they come to an agreement directly, without a judge.

Then someone is let off a great debt. The point is that he goes and lets his fellow human being off a much smaller debt.

A prodigal son comes home. He's welcomed by his father. But the decisive question is: will his older brother also accept him?

It's true that there are many parables about workers and their recompense which have quite different points from our parable. In them the workers in fact appear only in relation to the employer, and not in relation to one another. But the distinguishing feature of our particular parable is that it's ultimately about our relationship to one another. That's what's special about it. And as the inhabitants of this one parable we should be proud of that. We're only ideas of our creator. But with us, the focus of his thoughts is that in the end we should practise towards one another that justice and goodness which the owner has shown to us.'

The parable people are by no means reassured. They grumble: 'This point asks too much of us parable people. It's a utopia which explodes the laws of our parable world. No one has ever made voluntarily gifts in order to create a balance, so that jobs, recompense, security against hunger, sickness and accidents are shared. That doesn't work.'

The parable steward can only extricate himself by saying:

'Keep calm, dear parable people, indeed we're only ideas of our creator. We bear a message; not, however, to ourselves but to others. It's a message to real people, a message which can be realized only in the real world. Our parable world can remain as it is. Don't worry, there won't be a revolution here. No one needs to give anything up. But each one of us is part of a message to the real world. We tell people there: "You're all far more dependent on love and goodness than you really deserve and than you would concede. That's also true of your relationship to your creator. And it's true of your relationship to one another." It follows from this that among real people there is an obligation to give voluntarily, to balance out different opportunities in life. I know that something like that is too much to ask of our well-ordered, beautiful world of parables. But our creator didn't mean it to be too much for the real world. He entrusted it to real people.'

With this explanation the steward satisfies everyone. They all find it tremendously illuminating. For as we know, the good and the moral is always particularly illuminating if one can formulate it as a demand to others.

So all in all there is no rest in the world of parables. But individuals there still have problems. One comes forward and says: 'I'm the unfortunate individual whom the owner singles out and criticizes at the end. Many people grumbled, but he rebuked only me. You've just claimed that each one of us is part of a great message. And that we're all ideas of our creator. But why was I invented? Just to be pushed forward? Just to be criticized?' The steward replies: 'If you were singled out of the crowd, be proud of it. Something new always begins with individuals – even in a group, even in society. An individual has to begin. And you were made because you're this individual with whom the new can begin. You weren't put forward to show up your grumpiness, but because you've been given the best of all roles that one can have in this world: to begin on repentance, to begin on the new justice.'

When other parable people hear this, they too feel

encouraged to raise critical questions about the meaning of their personal existence. Now we hear the voice of the many who are among neither the first nor the last. They complain that people always talk only about the first, who toiled at the beginning of the day, and the last, who began work shortly before the end of the day. 'Very little,' they comment, 'is said about us. We play only a subsidiary role. Aren't we superfluous? Couldn't the parable dispense with us? What significance do we have?'

The parable steward answers patiently: 'You too are indispensable. If there were only the first and the last, then a stereotyped way of thinking would gain the upper hand. In the real world there are many people who know only black and white, good and evil, Germans and foreigners, left and right. All these are stereotypes, simplifications. Unfortunately real people have a weakness; they don't really perceive reality. They don't see the many transitional stages between the opposites. You're the intermediaries who should aim to help people to think about these transitional stages. You should train people to see that others aren't just black and white, left-wing and right-wing; there are many who don't fit into such pigeon-holes. So don't be bothered about your subsidiary role. You have one of the most important roles in the world: propagating and depicting a farewell to thinking in black and white.'

At the end all the parable people ask the steward: 'Why do you exist? Really, you're superfluous. In the morning the owner himself went to the market to hire workers. The parable wouldn't be much different if he also gave out the wages at the end.' Here the parable steward scratches his parable head. He hasn't thought much about this. It's always hardest to have to discover the meaning of one's quite personal existence. But he finds an answer: 'Our creator certainly engaged us all directly and gave us all directly a task for this parable life. He took us into service directly. But when it comes to a just and fair recompense for this, he depends on fellow workers among us parable people. Then he needs us. At least one of us. Among all the workers he needs a steward. In our parable world the recompense has to be shared out among us and not just beyond our parable world. Our creator thought me up to recall this.'

In the end everyone in the parable world is content. In it they all have a right to existence and all have a value. The parable world is intrinsically coherent and meaningful.

I shall now attempt to emerge from this beautiful parable world again. My question is: How are things with us? We're a bit of the real world. This real world isn't at all coherent and meaningful. This world is disrupted by the parables. They introduce a rift, cause dissatisfaction. The greatest parable-teller of modern literature, Franz Kafka, expressed this in the form of a parable about parables. Here it is in full:

> Many people complain that the words of the wise are time and again only parables, unusable in everyday life, which is all we have. When the wise man says 'Go over', he doesn't mean us to go over to the other side, which we could still do if it were worth the effort; he is referring to some legendary other side that we do not know, and which even he will not describe in more detail. So he cannot help us at all here. All these parables simply convey that the incomprehensible cannot be comprehended, and we knew that. We toil every day over other things.
>
> Thereupon someone says, 'Why do you resist? If you were to follow the parables, you yourselves would have become parables and thus free from daily toil.' Another says, 'I bet that's also a parable.' The first says, 'You've won.' The second says, 'But unfortunately only in the parable.' The first says, 'No, in reality; in the parable you've lost.'

How are we to understand this? Let's make clear to ourselves once again the difference between the parable world and the real world. Parable people have a great advantage: everything about them is full of meaning and significance. Their existence is eternal – just as they have been existing for two thousand years in the parables of Jesus. Real people are transitory. But they have another advantage: they are people of flesh and blood. Or as we say, they really exist.

The task of the parable is to take us from the real world into the world of parables. When have we won here, and when have we lost?

We have won when as real people we experience what parable people have in superfluity, namely meaning, not just in dreams and literary works. For them, everything has a meaning, a value. Everything is taken up and embedded in an overall outline with an artistic form. Parable people may be certain that they are ideas of their creator. We real people are never so sure about ourselves. All that is certain is that in about 150 years everyone here in this room will be dead. It is certain that we will often doubt whether everything has a meaning. But all that would be overcome if we ourselves became a parable. We will have won if we too understand ourselves as the ideas of a creator.

We will have won if we have an inkling that our life contains a message – to us and through us and for others; if we become certain that the creator of our life wants to say something through us: and he needs us for that. He also needs little things in our lives. We will have won if we become certain that between life and death we represent something as indestructible as the meaning of a figure in a parable, if we understand our life as an idea of God which we may think through further; in short, if we ourselves become a meaningful parable.

But from this one parable of the labourers in the vineyard we can learn that we will have won if we can join in realizing that justice which encounters us in it. We will have won if we do not live at the expense of others, but if in our own strength we achieve a balance which corresponds to the unconditional value of each individual human life, a balance which in parable form points to the equality of all human beings.

Of course we're a long way from that. History drives us in a different direction. The rich become richer and the poor poorer. Soon the rich among us will be gathering together in their enclaves with comprehensive security arrangements and private patrols – and the poorest will live elsewhere, some of them full of fury and hatred at all those who are successful and can live an ordered life. And because their desperate action threatens all of us, all of us will be all too ready to pay more for the police. We have already been able to observe world-wide, in the relationship between nation states, what is taking place within our society. The rich industrial countries are collaborating in setting up barriers against the tremendous pressure of immigration caused by the unequal distribution of goods and opportunities in life. And they are warding off those who knock on our doors because they are persecuted, and simply want to save their lives.

At the same time the poorest countries are gradually sinking into war, chaos and misery. It will become more and more difficult to secure to justice between those at the top and those at the bottom, between uppermost levels of society and the many who are impoverished, between the fully employed and the unemployed, between East and West, North and South. And precisely for that reason it will become increasingly necessary. We will have won only when time and again we bring about in the real world a movement towards that righteousness which first gives meaning and significance to life.

And when will we have lost? We will have lost when we dream of this righteousness only in parables and literary works, but do not realize anything of it in reality. We will have lost when time and again we do not win over real people to a vision of greater justice – and to the reality of a movement in this direction. For once individuals or whole groups come to the conclusion that there is no justice, and that it makes no sense to devote oneself to it in the real world, they withhold their own inner loyalty to human society. Then they say, 'Anything goes.' Then only the right of the stronger prevails. Then there is only the real world – and its completely parabolic significance disappears.

We theologians have always interpreted the parables in different ways, above all in terms of how much reality or how much poetry they contain. It would be just as important to change reality in the direction of becoming a parable: a parable of justice. We don't need to produce a perfect world, a paradise on earth, to do this. We need only set up signs which point as a parable to a greater justice. We will have won if our lives become a search for justice, if they make this message as vivid as a parable. We will have won if we become a parable with the message, 'Blessed are those who hunger and thirst for righteousness. They shall be filled.'

This Bible study was written for the Kirchentag in Leipzig on 21 June 1997. The Japanese mentioned at the beginning is Y. Watanabe. I have described his thoughts on Matt. 20.1–6 and the value of human beings in Buddhism and Christianity on the basis of his sketches, cf. Y. Watanabe, 'Selbstwertanalyse und christlicher Glaube', *EvTh* 40, 1980, 58–74. Kafka's parable has the title 'On the Parables'; it appears in F. Kafka, *Die Erzählungen*, Frankfurt am Main 1961, 328.

The Vicarious Death of Jesus

Interpreted for evangelical and modern Christians

(Mark 10.42–45)

And Jesus called them to him and said to them, 'You know that those who are supposed to rule over the Gentiles lord it over them, and their great men exercise authority over them. But it shall not be so among you; but whoever would be great among you must be your servant, and whoever would be first among you must be slave of all. For the Son of man also came, not to be served but to serve, and to give his life as a ransom for many.'

For many Christians this text is a central text. I keep finding that it speaks to Christians of opposed types of piety. It is a favourite text for evangelicals and liberals, for conservative Christians and liberation theologians. An evangelical Christian hears in it the message that Jesus came to give his life as a ransom for the many. For him the vicarious death of Jesus is the decisive thing. By contrast a liberal Christian with social commitments hears the message that the community should be an alternative society to the world in which the powerful oppress people. The text protests against repressive force. But we have understood the text only when we relate both of these: when the vicarious death of Jesus becomes a protest against political power, and when repressive power becomes the key to the vicarious death of Jesus.

So let's read the text in both perspectives. First let's ask: Why is the death of Jesus a protest against repressive power among men and women? Why does he have a social and political significance? We can recognize that more easily if we become clear that power constitutes power as the capacity to harm others to one's own advantage. It is the uncanny capacity to foist on others costs that one should be paying oneself. With the image of 'costs' we get close to the text. It speaks of the 'ransom', i.e. the economic costs of the freedom of a person, and does so in connection with political power and a personal fellowship with Jesus. The text thus speaks about three aspects of power: political, economic and personal power.

Political power is power which can compel others to risk their own lives. Every army, even the most democratic, is based on the principle that some can give the orders and others must sacrifice their lives for higher ends.

Economic power consists in being able to exploit others in such a way that they bear the 'costs' which one would otherwise have had to pay. Anyone who can foist costs on others has economic power – and any battle over tariffs is a struggle for this power. Who is foisting the cost on whom?

Power in our personal relationships is the most uncanny. Everyone knows how even the most intensive form of personal tie in partnerships is often exploited shamelessly: not only economically, but also psychologically and immaterially – by persuading a partner to sacrifice all thought of a career or by suppressing justified interests. It is uncanny because we are often unaware of it. Human ties often makes some people gladly do what apart from such ties would be sheer exploitation – and even with such a tie is the exercise of power.

We all live at the expense of others in this way. Our most intimate relationships are as little free from it as our political situations. Here we encounter one of the basic structures of life. But with Jesus another life becomes visible, a life which is no longer at the expense of other life, but which shares in the costs of another life, makes other life possible, and frees and promotes other life. Hence the message for conservative Christians is: Hold firm to the vicarious death of Jesus, but hear in him the protest against human exercise of power.

But now the text can also be read in another perspective. Our question is: Why does the whole world cry out for someone vicariously to take its misery upon himself – as a ransom for many?

Here's an illustration. Imagine a family in which relationships have broken down. Each is exploiting the other in a subtle way – living under the cloak of a false family solidarity at the expense of the other.

One member of the family becomes an alcoholic. First of all he seems to be the one who is weak, depressive and in need of help. All the others try to conceal his alcoholism from the public; they spare him the confrontation with reality, and become co-alcoholics. They don't notice how the one sick and weak person is manipulating and directing them, how precisely through his illness and weakness he is exercising power. Behind the semblance of a caring family, hidden aggressions, fury, disillusionment grow – on all sides.

Violence often breaks out in such families, above all where there is a family tradition of violence: where the father beats his wife and his children – and these in turn fight among themselves. Here too everything is concealed. No one must know about it, especially if alcohol is involved. Suppose that in such a family someone appears who stands outside the system of reciprocal violence and manipulation. Won't this person necessarily become the catalyst who discloses the relationships of violence which are denied? Won't the family tend to see him as a disturber of the peace, who destroys its fragile equilibrium? Won't it throw him out? Won't he vicariously attract all the violence that the members of the family practise towards one another?

But the entry of this new member into the broken family can also lead to a turning point. Only now does it dawn on everyone how entangled they are in a hopeless hatred of one another. All become conscious of their collective misery. And the longing awakens in everyone to live together in a different way.

Jesus assumed the role of the catalyst of repressed and denied violence in the human family. He drew the aggression of all upon himself. He also drew upon himself the aggression of those who wanted to overcome their awareness of such aggression, that of the pious and the righteous. In this way his death reveals not salvation, but our disastrous situation, the hopeless fragmentation of our relationships – and precisely that is the presupposition of a move towards salvation.

That is the message for modern Christians – for all who shrink from statements about the vicarious death of Jesus: the vicarious death of Jesus rightly stands at the centre of Christian faith. It makes us aware of the lostness of human beings, their hostility in matters great and small. But Christian faith lives by the fact that the inhumanity of human beings which manifests itself in the cross is not the last word. Christian faith lives by the power of the resurrection. Easter is a protest against our wanting to live at the expense of other life. Easter is a protest again being ready to let others suffer and die for us instead of standing up for them vicariously.

So my last word is a message for both sides, for both conservative and modern Christians. Those who have allowed themselves to be transformed by the power of the cross *and* the resurrection are free to intercede vicariously for others. Here are two examples. They are undramatic examples, deliberately taken from everyday life.

The first example involves suspicion and interceding for those who are suspected. We all need vicarious help here. Even the most innocent cannot defend themselves against some suspicions. Whatever they say can be interpreted in their situation as covering themselves. Whatever they do not say can be interpreted as a confession of guilt. Such people need others to intercede for them. Only such intercession can often protect them from loss of respect and honour.

The second example is worship. When we come together as a small group to pray and praise God, we act vicariously for people who cannot do that. They cannot do it because the bitterness of life has robbed them of belief in God. Or because disappointments with Christians have destroyed their trust in Christianity. Here too, for them acting vicariously means intervening against false suspicions about them. The many people who inwardly are not in a position to celebrate this worship are often not bad people, and we are certainly no better than they.

The Vicarious Death of Jesus

So let's intercede before God for them. Let's bear witness before God to all the love that we have received through them. In this way we become disciples of Jesus. He did not come to serve the pious but to serve all. He died not only for us but for the many, for the whole world, including those who find no access to him. He gave us his peace – not only for us, but for the whole world.

May this peace of God which surpasses all our understanding keep your hearts and minds in Christ Jesus. Amen.

This sermon was given at the Wednesday morning service in St Peter's Church, Heidelberg on 18 January 1995. I found helpful thoughts on the vicarious death of Jesus in R. Spaemann, 'Über den Sinn des Leidens', in *Einsprüche. Christliche Reden*, Einsiedeln 1977, 166–33, and J. Zink, *Sieh nach den Sternen – gibt acht auf die Gassen. Erinnerungen*, Stuttgart 1992, 125–31.

'Jesus of Nazareth, King of the Jews'

A Good Friday meditation on Christianity and Judaism

(Mark 15.24–27)

And they crucified him, and divided his garments among them, casting lots for them, to decide what each should take. And it was the third hour, when they crucified him. And the inscription of the charge against him read, 'The King of the Jews.' And with him they crucified two robbers, one on his right and one on his left.

In around the year 30 by our reckoning the Romans executed three men in front of the gates of Jerusalem. Two were rebels or ordinary criminals. Even at that time the third was regarded as a special case. After a denunciation by the Jewish aristocracy, the Roman prefect Pontius Pilate had condemned him to death. Pilate could not have known that three hundred years later the Roman empire in whose name he acted would recognize this third victim as a decisive mediator of salvation. He could not have guessed that this execution, which he had ordered as a repressive measure against the Jewish people, would one day become the most poisonous source of prejudice against this people – because of the false accusation that not he but 'the Jews' had executed this third victim.

On the placard which gave the grounds for his crucifixion was written 'the King of the Jews'. His tormented end was meant to be a public documentation of his failure. Nevertheless, this figure entered the cultural memory of humankind and posed the task of relating the salvation and disaster associated with him – the power of forgiveness and the destructive power of prejudices. For some the religious salvation bound up with the cross is a cloak for life-threatening prejudices; for others it is an opportunity to work through the mistakes governed by prejudice which have deeply distorted our culture. No wonder that our society is ambivalent towards this figure. The dispute as to whether he may be present in Bavarian schools as a crucifix or in schools in Brandenburg as a reminder to provide a guide in life is merely a symptom of this uncertainty.

Prejudice was involved from the start. That is evident from a retelling of the events. The residence of the then prefect of Judaea was Caesarea, on the Mediterranean. He went to Jerusalem with his soldiers only at the great festivals, for on festivals time and again there was unrest. His soldiers were recruited from the non-Jewish population of Palestine, and because of their origin they were anti-Jewish. Until the appearance of the Romans in 63 BC, Jewish kings from the house of the Hasmoneans had been their rulers. They must have felt the Jewish longing for their own king, who would renew rule over all Palestine, as a threat. When a Jewish king, Agrippa I, 41–44 CE, succeeded for a while in ruling over all Palestine, it was too much for them. After his sudden death they organized celebrations in Caesarea. They seized the statues of his daughters and put them on the roofs of brothels, to mock him and his family. That happened fifteen years after soldiers of the same cohort had mocked another 'king of the Jews' in no less macabre a way: the condemned man was given the insignia of a king, a purple cloak and a crown of thorns, together with a sceptre, and they knelt before him to pay homage to him as 'king of the Jews'. There is no doubt that Jesus was scorned, mocked and executed by representatives of an ancient anti-semitism. Ethnic conflicts in Palestine between Jews and non-Jews, along with conflicts between Roman and Jewish leaders on the one hand and the Jewish people on the other, were expressed in his death.

So already on the historical Good Friday prejudice was at work, but even more so in subsequent history. In a mediaeval chronicle we read of the French king Philippe-Auguste: 'He had heard very often . . . and had it firmly stamped on his memory, that the Jews in Paris each year on Good Friday or during Holy Weak secretly slaughtered a victim in underground caves . . .'

This absurd accusation of ritual murder on Good Friday served as a pretext in 1181 to confiscate the property of all Jews. The historical Jesus, who himself was victim of ancient hostility towards the Jews, had meanwhile become the church's Christ, who could be played off against Jews. Time and again Good Friday was an occasion for making Jews victims of Christian anti-Judaism. Modernity handed down the traditional antipathy to Jews on a new basis. The religious basis of the prejudice was first replaced by racist, then by anti-Zionist motives. But the poison of antisemitism has still not yet been overcome.

Precisely for that reason, the remembrance of Good Friday is necessary. The symbol of the cross and of Good Friday irrevocably bind our culture and Christian faith to Judaism. The insight that Jesus was crucified as a representative of Jewish hopes is part of the growing recognition that Jesus belongs to Judaism.

Christians and Jews are only hesitantly accepting that Jesus belongs to both religions. The hesitation of Jews is understandable, for they were often exposed to missionary pressure when they expressed sympathy and esteem for Jesus; it was the abandonment of missionary pressure in pluralistic societies which first created the possibility of a drawing together. Christians hesitate because they are afraid of losing their Christian identity if they don't mark Christianity off from Judaism. But there are already many Christians who find that a menorah (the seven-branched candlestick as a symbol of Judaism) in a church is an extension of their identity. Perhaps the churches should have begun on such symbolic teaching in their own buildings, regardless of whether it is possible in our school buildings – not least in order to free our contemporaries of the anxiety that in looking at a crucifix they were exposing themselves to 'missionary pressure', as our Supreme Court thought. Here too, only a credible demonstration of renunciation of any missionary pressure gives the freedom for a new approach to this central symbol of our culture – as a remembrance of its Jewish roots, which precisely for that reason is more than a random reminiscence of cultural history. It still indicates the obligation to overcome the poison of antisemitism and to practise solidarity with the failures and the victims of violence and injustice. This historical and ethical symbolic content of the cross doesn't require impossible confessions of anyone. Our society and our culture become poorer if we exclusively subordinate the cross and Good Friday to a church subculture. At the centre of our culture stands a symbol which impressively says that truth and right can stand on the side of the victims and the failures. At the centre of the Christian religion stands the statement that a victim of state violence and ethnic conflicts is the basis for orientation in life. God identifies himself with him, and through him with all victims of violence and prejudice. For his followers the Easter experience was more powerful than the experience of his failure – an abiding protest against those who believe that the weak and the defeated have no chance.

This Good Friday meditation appeared in the *Frankfurter Allgemeine Zeitung* on 4 April 1996. For the action of the French king Philippe-Auguste (1180–1223) against the Jews see B.Blumenkranz, in K.H. Rengstorf and S.von Kortzfleisch, *Kirche und Synagoge. Handbuch zur Geschichte von Juden und Christen. Darstellung mit Quellen*, 1, Stuttgart 1968, 127–9.

Waiting for God in the Wilderness of Life

An Advent sermon

(Luke 3.1–14)

In the fifteenth year of the reign of Tiberius Caesar, Pontius Pilate being governor of Judaea, and Herod being tetrarch of Galilee, and his brother Philip tetrarch of the region of Ituraea and Trachonitis, and Lysanias tetrarch of Abilene, in the high-priesthood of Annas and Caiaphas, the word of God came to John the son of Zechariah in the wilderness. And he went into all the region about the Jordan, preaching a baptism of repentance for the forgiveness of sins. As it is written in the book of the words of Isaiah the prophet, 'The voice of one crying in the wilderness: Prepare the way of the Lord, make his paths straight. Every valley shall be filled, and every mountain and hill shall be brought low, and the crooked shall be made straight, and the rough ways shall be made smooth; and all flesh shall see the salvation of God.' John said to the multitudes that came out to be baptized by him, 'You brood of vipers! Who warned you to flee from the wrath to come? Bear fruits that befit repentance, and do not begin to say to yourselves, "We have Abraham as our father"; for I tell you, God is able from these stones to raise up children to Abraham. Even now the axe is laid to the root of the trees; every tree therefore that does not bear good fruit is cut down and thrown into the fire.'

And the multitudes asked him, 'What then shall we do?' And he answered them, 'He who has two coats, let him share with him who has none; and he who has food, let him do likewise.' Tax collectors also came to be baptized, and said to him, 'Teacher, what shall we do?' And he said to them, 'Collect no more than is appointed you.' Soldiers also asked him, 'And we, what shall we do?' And he said to them, 'Rob no one by violence or by false accusation, and be content with your wages.'

Advent is a time of expectation. In it the Bible becomes a

textbook of expectation. It asks, 'What may we expect in life? What is coming to us?' And it says, 'What comes to us in life is not this or that, but God himself.' We expect too little if we do not wait on him. We still don't have the right expectation if we fail to notice that we are without him in the dark hours of our life. We are wrong if we do not detect that his presence has touched us in joy. Above all, we have illusions if we think that this expectation isn't risky. On the contrary, it leads us into the wilderness – into a wilderness beyond life, beyond society, beyond our familiar self.

The great teacher of this expectation is John the Baptist. He calls us into the wilderness, there to wait for God. And my task today will also be to call your thoughts and imagination into the wilderness – on three excursions.

The first excursion takes us to the frontiers of life. Only once in my life have I seen the wilderness, in Syria. Wherever you look, you see sand, stones, an infinitely wide horizon, dead matter eroded by a hot wind, but in which life is concealed. When you return to villages and towns, with greenness, people and houses, you become aware that the human world in which we live consists merely of small islands in a giant lifeless cosmos. But a tremendous energy is invested in these islands. And on them the mosques in turn form little islands on the island: places of coolness and clarity in the midst of the heat of the day. I love these mosques. In their strictness, simplicity and lack of images they remind me of the Reformed churches which are familiar from my childhood days on. I loved to sit on the floor in mosques and think. And it dawned on me that the people who worship God here time and again in their prayers unite them-selves with that tremendous energy which wills human life – life in the middle of the wilderness, life threatened by the wilder-ness. And they radiate the certainty that the creator wants all this: the wilderness and life, and above all life in the wilderness and despite the wilderness.

Now in Syria I experienced not only the wilderness but for the first time in my life also shootings, little political skirmishes which probably didn't find their way into any news broadcasts. Sunnis were fighting Shiites and vice versa. It was uncanny. When the first shots were fired, the people fled into the houses. The streets emptied in a flash. The tension could be felt in the town for a long time afterwards, in tighter control by the army and the police. And I had a new topic to meditate on in the mosques: isn't this small human world threatened even more from the inside than from the outside – threatened by our inability to live together, by religious fanaticism, by national-isms, by the stupid rejection of those who are different?

And I heard the voice of John the Baptist within me. He said: 'Don't imagine that nothing could happen to you because you are descended from *Homo Sapiens* and tower above other creatures by virtue of a cerebrum. Perhaps you are only a dead branch of the tree of evolution. Perhaps it will soon have to be chopped off, because it brings forth bad fruit, because it's a mistake. Hasn't the axe already been laid to the root of the tree? Why shouldn't creation begin again with pre-living struc-tures? Why shouldn't new life develop from stones and dead matter?'

I didn't find it difficult to imagine our relationship to the whole of reality in the image of a judgment, as John the Baptist did. We live as if under a harsh threat of punishment: if we develop forms of life which contradict the basic conditions of reality, if we do not convert in time, then a merciless judgment will come upon us. John the Baptist and kindred apocalyptic seers saw that centuries ago in their visions – but they also introduced hope into their images, hope that failure can be averted.

If you meditate like this on the edge of the wilderness, on the frontier between death and life, and affirm life as an island in a lifeless cosmos, then you have made a first basic decision: a decision for the experiment of human culture – for risky life in the wilderness of the cosmos and despite this wilderness. And if it dawns on you when confronted with people praying in mosques, synagogues and churches that this basic decision is the echo of a prior decision for life, then God has come. Then his will for creation has also seized you. You've heard his voice. Then what God expects of you becomes important – like all that you've expected of him. But the voice says even more.

For this I must lure your thoughts and imaginations on a second excursion into the wilderness. This time it's into the wilderness of Judaea, where John the Baptist is at work. He was a remarkable fellow, so remarkable that Luke leaves out the description of his exotic appearance given by Mark.

His clothing, camel hair and a leather girdle, was a protest against those who wore fine garments in the palaces of the rulers.

His food, locusts and wild honey, was a protest against the banquets celebrated by his ruler Herod (here, though, it needs to be added that some New Testament scholars regard locusts roasted in honey as a delicacy).

His abode was the wilderness, which in the Jordan valley looks inhospitable, but which is broken by the Jordan and its narrow stream.

We all know such figures: sympathetic fellows with beards, baggy shirts, sandals and organic food. The outfit already conveys the message: Your life-style is all wrong. They put our life-style in question with gentle moral aggression.

Should we learn from John the Baptist to hear God's call in such outsiders? Should we wait for God there, among drop-outs on the fringe of society? But how do we distinguish them from layabouts, demagogues and con-men? There were already such people at that time. There were prophets who promised signs and wonders in the wilderness and led many people to destruction. There was the Qumran community which referred to the same text of Isaiah as John the Baptist, 'In the wilderness prepare the way of the Lord', and which withdrew from the evil world to wait for the great battle at the end of days when with their help and God's help all the children of darkness would be slaughtered.

Had Luke had prophetic gifts, he could have forecast yet others who would lead people astray: men with business suits and good manners, who at the end of the twentieth century present to camera the message:

> The voices of those who cry in prosperity!
> Bar the way in our land,
> so that others may remain in the desert.
> Dig deep the trenches and raise high the barriers,
> so that no one can get through to you
> when they are fleeing persecution and threat.
> Instruct the toll collectors to turn them away,
> and the soldiers to track them down,
> that the whole human race may see
> what a humane country we are –
> we who grant exile to anyone who is really persecuted
> – in neighbouring countries.

Had Luke with prophetic foresight already known such deeply problematical sayings, he would have had one more reason to expand Mark's account of John the Baptist at a decisive point. In Mark, John the Baptist had already applied Isaiah's saying to himself:

> The voice of one crying in the wilderness,
> make ready the way of the Lord,
> make his paths straight.

Luke quotes the Isaiah saying more fully. He adds

> Every valley shall be filled,
> and every mountain and hill shall be brought low,
> and the crooked shall be made straight,
> and the rough ways shall be made smooth;
> and all flesh shall see the salvation of God.

With this sentence of the Isaiah saying Luke breaks off. For this is what is decisive for him, what distinguishes prophets from demagogues and con-men. The salvation of which the true prophet speaks is for the whole world. It is for 'all flesh', i.e. for the whole human race. It is not just for his own people but for all peoples. Any prophet who promises salvation only for his own people – against other peoples and to their detriment – isn't a true prophet. God's salvation is for all, or it isn't God's salvation.

Now one could say that that's true of God's salvation. We're happy to share our religious faith with all, but not bread and butter. The salvation of which Luke speaks is a spiritual salvation. It has nothing to do with politics and social equality.

One could think that Luke foresaw such objections. For unlike Mark he embeds his account of John the Baptist in a political framework. He begins by dating John's appearance with the help of five rulers and two church politicians. One after another he mentions:

– the emperor Tiberius;
– Pontius Pilate, the prefect of Judaea;
– Herod, the Roman client prince over Galilee;
– Philip, who reigned over parts of present-day Jordan;
– Lysanias, a further client prince, who ruled over parts of present-day Lebanon;
– and the two high priests Annas and Caiaphas.

One can't put it much more clearly: note, readers and hearers, that a figure is now appearing who has something to do with politics.

It is in keeping with this at the end Luke makes John the Baptist go beyond what he says in Mark about the practical consequences of repentance.

First, the people are to share. Those who have two garments are to give one away. The same applies to butter and bread.

Secondly, the toll-collectors, who at that time collected not only tolls but taxes, are not to be corrupt.

Thirdly, the soldiers (who at that time were also the police) are not to plunder and extort.

In other words, those who have fiscal and military power are not to exploit the weaker ones. Here once again we encounter politics, now not at the top level, but lower down, in the form of toll collectors and soldiers, in the form of people who implement government rule – the rule of the emperor Tiberius, of Pontius Pilate, of Herod – on the ground.

Moreover Luke doesn't have a positive picture of these rulers. He regards Herod as a villain. For shortly after the text of this sermon he writes: 'To all the evil things that Herod had done he added this, that he shut up John in prison.' The outcome of this story is well known.

So we are to go into the wilderness to this prophet, to wait for God. And by that I understand that there we must distance ourselves from our society, from the distribution of opportunities in life which is so familiar to us. As long as we live in our society, it seems to us to be normal. But when we look at our society from outside, from the perspective of the wilderness, we can only be horrified at the great difference of opportunities – already in our own country between East and West, but even more between the developed states and the rest of the world. No one has patent recipes for really fighting such inequality in the world. But it would be cynical to accept it as unavoidable. It would be cynical to let hunger go on biting, not only in Somalia but in many places.

Here a second basic decision is required of us. The first was a decision on human culture generally. The second is made in the midst of it: the decision for the weaker ones and those who do not get their share. If we recognize that this decision too is only the echo of a greater will, then God has come among us. Then his will for the poor and the weak has also embraced us. Then what he expects of us will become more important to us than anything that we expect of him. But his will requires yet more of us.

I want to take your thoughts yet a third time into the wilderness, or more precisely to the Jordan: through the midst of the wilderness. There John the Baptist calls for repentance, for baptism. He calls everyone to baptism, each individually. He calls everyone to become different.

But can people become different? Here John uses a bold

metaphor, though we no longer hear it like that: he requires fruits of repentance. He requires them of people whom he compares with trees which are to be cut down because they do not bear fruit. But how is a tree to repent? How is it to bring forth better fruit? Biblical thought on this is more sceptical elsewhere. A good tree brings forth good fruit and a bad tree bad fruit. That's that. And that's how it always will be. Or have you ever seen a tree convert? Can it change its behaviour? John the Baptist opposes such scepticism: if God can make children out of stones, then he can make new people out of old. And for that he offers baptism – as an indelible seal indicating that we have been born to be reborn. That we aren't finished. That we can and may become different.

And that is precisely why he calls us into the wilderness to begin our lives anew there – where we have left behind our familiar roles, all that has accrued to us, our competence, our status, our firm expectations and our well-established disillusionments. He calls us from what we have become. Everyone pays a price for growing up. Recently, when I was thumbing through the notebooks which I filled with all kinds of profound thoughts between the ages of fifteen and twenty – and to read them again after thirty years requires a good deal of empathy towards oneself – I came across a note which I liked: Becoming a character probably means throwing away nine of the ten characters that are in one. One never becomes a character without losses. Everyone has an inner jumble room containing the things that have not been developed – a bit of wilderness in ourselves. But we have to go into it if we want to begin again in the midst of life. There could be an idea of God there which we might still think through to the end.

But perhaps I needn't invite you into this private wilderness. Perhaps you're already in the middle of it.

Perhaps an illness has removed you from normal life. Perhaps a separation has cast you into deep depression.

Perhaps an experience of injustice has hurt and disturbed you.

Perhaps you are constantly aware that your best plans have failed.

Perhaps you despise yourself because you're no longer what you once wanted to be.

Perhaps you've reached the end of life and with death comes the flat feeling, 'Was that all?'

In that case no one needs to call you into the wilderness. You're already in the midst of it.

In that case, though, hear the message of John the Baptist as comfort, as a voice in the midst of the wilderness of your life. There, in the wilderness, prepare the way of the Lord. He's coming there. He's looking for you there. And even if you think that the roots of your life are already withered and everything is tottering, if you feel that the axe is already laid to them, even then, indeed particularly then, the message of John the Baptist applies to you. You can become free of the burden of the past; you can become new. God is always ready to see the new person in you. God is ready to take a small part of the new for the whole. He is ready to think what was mistaken in your life through to a good end.

In that case you've made a third basic decision. Not only a decision for a weak and questionable culture in the wilderness of the cosmos; not only a decision for the weak and questionable ones in this culture but also a decision for the weak and questionable things in yourself. If you become conscious that you too are furthering a greater will, then you will no longer be a poor thing, for then you will be choosing to think through God's thoughts in your life to the end, to complete his quest for what is lost, including his quest for what is lost in you.

Advent is a time of expectation. In it we are called into the wilderness, to wait for God anew. We set out in the expectation that God will build the way for our life. But God wants us to prepare the way for him. If we allow ourselves to be seized totally by this expectation, by this will for a humane life, for the weak among us and the weakness in us – then we prepare his way in this world. Together with John the Baptist. John was not a Christian. A Jew and a Muslim could also say everything that he said. So we are to prepare the way for God in this world along with Muslims and Jews, along with them and with John the Baptist, not against them. And if this way takes us through Nazareth, we should accept Jesus as our brother, as a brother who teaches us to live with other brothers and sisters in our Father's house – also with Muslims and Jews: here in the Federal Republic and in Bosnia, in Syria, in Israel and throughout the world.

And may the peace of God which surpasses our understanding keep our hearts and minds in Christ Jesus. Amen.

A sermon given on 13 December 1992 in St Peter's Church, Heidelberg. The previous week the party leaders of the two largest German parties, W. Schäuble and U. Klose, had negotiated the 'asylum compromise' and presented it with great self-satisfaction on television. According to this the wording of the asylum law remained unchanged, but the right of asylum was refused to those who entered the Federal Republic of German through certain third countries – on the assumption that they could have found asylum in these third countries. As the Federal Republic is surrounded only by 'safe third countries', this compromise over asylum amounted to a far-reaching abolition of the right to asylum. A bit of sham – one might even call it a collective lie – has been accepted into the constitution. At the same time the murderous civil war between Muslims and Serbs in Bosnia increased the flow of refugees seeking refuge in Germany through the asylum law. So the cohabitation of Muslims and Christians was a topic of universal concern.

An Invitation to the Feast of Life

Or the decision between two kinds of happiness

(Luke 14.16–24)

But he said to him, 'A man once gave a great banquet and invited many; and at the time for the banquet he sent his servant to say to those who had been invited, "Come, for all is now ready." But they all alike began to make excuses. The first said to him, "I have bought a field, and I must go out and see it; please excuse me." And another said, "I have bought five yoke of oxen, and I need to try them out; please excuse me." And another said, "I have married a wife, and so I cannot come." Then the servant came and reported this to his master. The householder got angry and said to his servant, "Go out quickly to the streets and alleys of the city and bring in the poor and maimed and blind and lame."' And the servant said, "Sir, what you commanded has been done, and there is still room." Then the master said to the servant, "Go out to the highways and hedges, and compel people to come in, that my house may be filled. For I tell you, none of those men who were invited shall taste my banquet."'

Sometimes people like me get annoyed at the rising generation, because in it there are virtuosi in the art of making half-promises: 'Yes, I'll come as long as nothing crops up in the meantime.' Behind this there isn't the reservation that one could fall ill, or have an accident, or even be appointed a minister. Behind it is the simple reservation: perhaps there will be even more interesting invitations or prospects of more exciting experiences. Our parable reconciles me to these young people, since it shows that the problem has always existed. Someone arranges a meal. A first invitation goes out. A second follows immediately before the beginning of the meal in the evening. But all those who have been invited have something more interesting to do. Do they decline because urgent needs prevent them? Certainly not.

For example, the first person invited doesn't want to buy a field which he would lose if he didn't go for it immediately. He's already bought it. He's already seen it, since no one buys a field blind. But he wants to take another look. He wants to enjoy his new purchase once again.

The second person doesn't have a unique opportunity to buy ten oxen today. He's already bought them. Of course he inspected them first. No farmer buys oxen unseen. But he wants to try them out once again, to make sure that he's got a good buy.

The third person isn't getting married today. If he was, one could understand a refusal. He's already got married. This time, in contrast to the first two refusals, there is no indication in the parable of what he wants to do in the evening. There's a void in the text. It provokes the question: What are the newly married man's intentions? What does he want to try out? Certainly not a field, or oxen. Already at that time the hearers thought what we're all thinking: he wants to enjoy his wife.

So these aren't Puritan workaholics, people whose businesses leave them no time, top executives overwhelmed with deadlines. Here the alternatives aren't everyday concerns or a feast, duty or enjoyment. Here the alternatives are two kinds of enjoyment: real delights, but delights of different kinds.

Here a decision has to be made between the joys which every individual enjoys for himself or herself and shared joy. The field has only one owner. The oxen have only one master. The wife has only one husband. But the invitation is to a shared joy. It is an invitation to a feast which is meant to bring many people together.

Here a decision has to be made between the joys which each has achieved though his initiative and a joy which is given. The field has been bought, negotiations have been completed over the oxen, the wife has been wooed. But the host is inviting people to a joy which he is preparing – and which everyone else can only receive. Only one thing is asked of them: they have to accept the invitation and come along ready to rejoice.

So the question here is: which is the greater joy? A society which regards individual joy, joy which individuals have earned and achieved for themselves, as the supreme value becomes blind to a joy which is shared and given. But the greatest joy that can bind people together is joy in God. And that kind of joy can only be a gift. Its essence is that it's shared with others. It doesn't deprive anyone of anything. That is what the parable is talking about. It sets out to demonstrate the special character of this joy. And what is that? If I buy a field, no one else can buy it. If I marry a wife, perhaps someone else has been cheated of the fulfilment of his hopes. But when we rejoice at hearing God's call and accept his invitation, then we aren't taking anything away from anyone. Then our joy becomes all the greater if we share it with others. Then we aren't in competition but in conviviality – living together and sharing together.

But, many people will say, I don't notice that I've been invited to the feast of life. Life isn't a feast for me, it's a tragedy. Doesn't the invitation to a feast ask too much of all the unfortunates in this tragedy? Doesn't it make them feel all the more how much their lives have been damaged, how far removed they are from shared joy? Doesn't this invitation make many people sad?

Far from it: it is the unfortunate, the poor, the maimed, the blind and the paralysed in particular who are invited to God's feast. And they, of all people, are more sensitive to the call than others. They know that true joy can only be shared joy. For the paralysed depend on someone to carry them, the blind on someone to lead them, the poor on someone to help them. It is the poor and the toilers on this earth who have no problem in accepting joy which is given. Yet they must all do one thing themselves, even the poorest, the blind and the paralysed. They must all accept the invitation. No one can do that for another. We must each do it for ourselves. God's call goes out to each of us. And we are asked whether we accept it or not.

But who are we in this parable? Are we the successful people to whom rejoicing about individual success is more important than shared joy? Yes, we are. In our society we are all programmed to achieve and to seek satisfaction in our achievements. That's not wrong. But it isn't everything. There's an even greater joy. So let us hear God's call before we neglect the great joyful feast of life because of our petty joys.

Or are we the unsuccessful people who are poor, inwardly crippled, paralysed and blind? Yes, we're that as well. In our society there is a pressure always to seem positive, even if we feel quite different. There is probably no one who isn't damaged in some way. So let's hear God's call. It's addressed particularly to what is crippled, paralysed and blind in us.

Or are we the servant who delivers the call? He is rejected by some, but receives a surprising acceptance from others which no one would have expected. We are him, too. When we attempt to pass on God's invitation we all have this experience: we seem to be a burden on those whom we would most have liked to address. And we get a hearing where we wouldn't have expected it.

No matter what role we assume, the invitation has been given. It applies unconditionally. It applies to all. It also applies to you. You're meant. You're an idea of God. And only you can carry out this idea of God by accepting his invitation. No one can do it for you.

And to what feast has he invited you? The feast consists in your making contact with God; in your hearing his promise, 'I have called you by your name. You are mine'; in a spark of life falling into your life so that you sense that it glows in many other people, as it does in you. You aren't alone.

So when you hear this invitation, don't half-accept it. Don't think, 'Yes, I'll go if nothing else crops up; if I don't find anything more interesting; if I don't have to concentrate all my energy on my career.' When one begins to get satiated with the many things which now give pleasure, then perhaps it's time to seek other joys. For all other joys are unimportant – measured by the one great joy – a shared joy in God.

And may the peace of God which surpasses all our understanding keep your hearts and minds in Christ Jesus.

Signs of Life

This sermon was given at the Wednesday morning service in St Peter's Church, Heidelberg on 19 June 1996. The contrast between competition and conviviality is inspired by T. Sundermeier, 'Convivenz als Grundstruktur ökumenischer Existenz heute', in W. Hüber, D. Ritschl and T. Sundermeier, *Ökumenische Existenz heute* I, Munich 1986, 49–100.

Mustardseed Faith

A sermon for good people who have stopped believing

(Luke 17.5–6/Mark 11.22–24)

The apostles said to the Lord,

'Increase our faith!'
And the Lord said,
'If you had faith as a grain of mustardseed, you could say to this sycamore tree, "Be rooted up, and be planted in the sea," and it would obey you.'

In the Gospel of Mark we find another image. There Jesus says:

'Truly I say to you, whoever says to this mountain, "Be taken up and cast into the sea," and does not doubt in his heart, but believes that what he says will come to pass, it will be done for him.'

Our theme today is the power of faith, which is as small as a grain of mustardseed and yet moves mountains and uproots trees. Appealing to such faith, the Reformation once changed a whole world: the church and society of the late Middle Ages. Today one is tempted to preach less about the power of this faith than about its weakness. It often doesn't seem to be even the size of a grain of mustardseed. Those who preach faith are coming up against a time which is weary of faith. And there are many good people who feel quite comfortable in such a time. A modern writer expressed it like this in a short story about faith in a distant land:

To begin with, faith moved mountains only when it was absolutely necessary, so that for millennia the landscape remained unchanged. But when faith began to spread and people liked the idea of moving mountains, they did nothing

129

more than move them to and fro, and each time it became more difficult to rediscover them where they had been left the night before. Of course this situation created more problems than it solved. So the good people (in that land) preferred to give up faith, and now the mountains normally remained where they were. If there happens to be an earth tremor on the road which claims a few travellers as victims, it is because someone, somewhere, near or far, still had a remnant of faith.

I've asked myself how this story could go on. What happens in a land with good people who have given up faith? I imagine missionaries coming to this land to disseminate faith in it again.

The first missionary goes to work cautiously. For a long time he listens to the complaints about faith. What are they? The good people say that faith is socially destructive and keeps causing little earthquakes. For it tends towards fundamentalism and fanaticism. As an example they quote from their history how once for a few years they had been ruled over by a criminal mass movement and its leader. After seizing power these had proudly printed on commemorative postcards: 'Unyielding faith and a fanatical will for victory led to 30 January 1933.' After such experiences they are sceptical about any unconditional faith. Even if it becomes effective for social purposes, it remains an uncanny force. It could move mountains – but also destroy valleys and villages and bury them under avalanches. So they would prefer to stick to reason. And indeed their country has become a little more reasonable since there have been fewer of those people who for good or bad reasons keep saying, 'Here I stand, I can do no other.' They say that it's much easier to live with people who say, 'Here I stand, but I can adopt a different position, especially if it's more agreeable to you (and an advantage for me).'

Our missionary comes from the Basel Revelation Mission. So he exclaims, 'No, you're confusing religion and faith. Religion is all the unconditional and fanatical power which human beings mobilize to achieve their aims. Religion is human work. But faith is the work of God. God takes us into his service for his purposes. Religion is a terrible error. It causes immoral earthquakes, has heretics burned and sets crusades marching. It's a deeply godless affair. You're right to have turned away from it. The true faith which moves mountains and trees is something quite different.'

And then he embarks on a sharp attack on the reason to which the good people of the land have converted.

'Why do you complain about the ambiguity of religion? Don't you have the same problems with reason? I won't bring up its great excesses here – the terror against people and against nature that has been committed in its name. I merely want to point to the danger to reason from within, a danger which emerges in cultivated language, and in a very, very distinguished way.

Don't you know those excellent representatives of economic reason who bluntly declare, "I can't think socially, because I don't know what that means"?

Don't you know the lawyers who with all the solemnity of the Enlightenment say, "Law is a social technology – and has nothing to do with justice"?

Don't you know the social scientists who win peace prizes and Nobel prizes – and who with their acute reason once argued for compulsory sterilization to combat degeneracy and cut costs?

Don't you know all those smart scientists who with many lifelike anecdotes vividly describe how the quest for truth in our universities is in any case the chance by-product of career wishes? And they don't just intend that as satire, in order to oppose it powerfully. They think that this is how things are and must be.

Reason is endangered from within by cynicism. How quickly it gives up! How quickly it loses its self-respect! How easily it allows itself to be exploited!'

And then comes the great taunt from the vintage Protestant tradition, the taunt about the 'whore reason' who sells herself to anyone.

So far the good people have given our missionary a ready

hearing. But one of them who still has some knowledge of the Bible from his Christian period protests. 'You mock reason as a whore. But with Jesus I tell you that this whore will enter the kingdom of God before you pious people. Can't reason also convert? Isn't that its principle? Conversion, the constant revision of its own mistakes?' So the first attempt at mission was only a moderate success.

Therefore a second missionary was sent. He comes from the Munich Enlightenment Mission and at first glance his central message seems to meet the problem of the 'good people' precisely. He says, 'Faith by itself can be corrupted. You're right: it bears within it the possibility of fanaticism. This fanaticism isn't something that one can distinguish clearly from faith. But this faith which can become a curse can also become a blessing. For that to happen it must ally itself with reason and allow itself to be corrected by reason. But reason alone can also be corrupted. All too quickly it becomes cynical reason. It needs a faith which it cannot provide by itself, a faith that it has a task and a promise in this world. The solution lies in an alliance of faith and reason.' Of course this Munich Enlightenment missionary spoke to me straight from the heart. His mission too, seemed quite successful.

But then a disaster happened in the land of the good people. A car accident. A princess lost her life. People were devastated. For a while the dead princess was venerated almost in a religious way: hadn't she worked with AIDS victims and the victims of land-mines like a saint? Hadn't evil powers been against her? Couldn't everyone discover some of their problems in hers: affairs, depressions, addictions – and the attempt to make something of all this? And hadn't she opposed institutions rich in tradition when they had humiliated her? Even the reasonable people in the land were caught up in this – although of course they showed it only by analysing the effects on others. But hasn't it to be conceded that here irrational powers are at work, which cannot be grasped by an alliance of faith and reason?

Then a third missionary came to the country. He came from the Heidelberg Bible Mission. His methods were old-fashioned and his exegesis somewhat controversial, as Heidelberg exegesis is. Anyway, he sought inspiration above all in the Bible. And there he found a word of Paul's about faith which moves mountains. Paul says, '. . . and although I had all faith, so that I could move mountains, and had not love, I would be nothing'.

Here he found the key to the problem. The alliance of faith and reason is perhaps very good for writing clever books. But can it change people to their innermost depths? Can it change life? Can it develop a power to form community? Can it prevent the terrible derailments of both faith and reason? Why should this alliance be a combination of a narrow revelation theology which despises all human action and a cynical reason which offers highly-intelligent reasons for such scorn? Is that really the way to a faith which moves mountains but doesn't overwhelm villages and valleys; which uproots trees but doesn't turn land-scapes into deserts? A third power is needed, love. If faith is governed by the power of love, it cannot harm other people. Then it is preserved from fanaticism.

But even that doesn't solve all the problems. Love is vulnerable. Love scorned often turns into bitterness and hatred. How many people begin their lives in a spirit of love, but then come the disappointments, the blows, the injustices – and then they are hardened! Here's just one example.

Recently I heard of a very sympathetic woman who devoted her energies on behalf of some small children to the very limits. She was a great help to them and the family. She made it possible for the mother to be able to complete her professional training. She did something for the emancipation of a woman. But behind her back it was said of her – by the same people whom she helped: 'This old woman has an altruism complex which we must exploit. It will help her to cope better with her psychopathology.' Shouldn't we be angry at that? Can't such love rightly turn into bitterness?

While the good people were reflecting on love like this, an earthquake again shook the country. Had a faith that moves mountains again been active in the wrong place? Be this as it may, the rescue teams set off immediately to look for survivors in a landslide. Fortunately no one had come to harm. But they found a crucifix buried under the rubble and earth, and immediately the rumour went round the land that God himself had been overwhelmed, God himself had been buried.

What was to be done? It was decided to set the crucifix up again after three days – rejecting some constitutional objections that the sight of a crucifix might perhaps exert an illegitimate missionary pressure. For this reason, they didn't invite any of the missionaries to give a short sermon when the crucifix was set up again, but one of the old pastors who belonged to the minority in the land who had not given up their faith. What did he say?

Dear fellow citizens, dear brothers and sisters. Your faith will be overwhelmed and shaken time and again. But you should know that God also dies with your faith. And with God your faith will also rise again. For nothing has power over death but God himself.

Your faith has often died already – on the one hand because of external catastrophes, the many earth tremors which have buried other people, and on the other because of cynical ideas from within. Perhaps only a very little faith has remained, as tiny as a grain of mustardseed, almost invisible to our eyes. But this little, tiny faith can be very powerful.

Here is my defininition of this smallest possible, minimal, mustardseed faith. You have this faith if you say yes to your life. And with this yes you can achieve a great deal.

Perhaps you think that this is something that can be dealt with quite privately, between two persons. But many people aren't aware of everything that they include in this yes. Those who say yes, say yes to all the processes that have produced them: not just to parents and family, not just to this small earth, but also to the many stars which came into being and perished and allowed the system of elements to arise. If it is meaningful for me to exist, then it cannot be meaningless for something to exist and for everything to exist. The smallest grain of mustardseed faith contains a yes to all creation. With it begins a love related to all that is.

Furthermore, this yes contains a yes to other people. A grain of mustardseed can exist only in symbiosis with many minerals and plants, a human being only with other human beings. We can say 'I' only because other people have first said 'you' to us. And if no one has shown us respect, we cannot show respect to anyone else. This small mustardseed grain of faith remains dead unless much love is already hidden in it.

If we lose this little spark of faith – this yes to ourselves – then the whole world and all our fellow human beings sink into meaninglessness. But if we preserve it, everything becomes different. The mountains may not be moved, but we see them in a new light, as a piece of creation.

As long as you set up crucifixes in this land, it will be possible to hear the promise: your faith may be put to the test, may be tortured, tormented, crucified and buried. But when it is crucified and buried with Christ, you may trust that it will rise with him – so that you already change here and now into a new life. This faith is dead if it does not embrace love – love for all being, love for other human beings. And therefore what Paul wrote is true: ' . . . and although I had all faith, so that I could move mountains, and had not love, I would be nothing'. Faith, too, would be nothing. Only love can prevent people being overwhelmed by faith which moves mountains. Only love can ensure that the unconditional power of the faith that moves mountains does not become a curse, but a blessing.

And may the peace of God which surpasses all our understanding keep you in this love in Christ Jesus. Amen.

This sermon was preached in St Peter's Church, Heidelberg, on 7 September 1997. The short story about faith in a distant land comes form A. Monterosso, 'Der Glaube und die Berge', in L. Graf, U. Kabitz et al., *Die Blume des Blinden*, Munich 1985, no. 142, p.158. I have transferred the story to a distant land to make the construction of a mission in this land possible. I have taken the Nazi motto from a com-memorative postcard of 1933, depicted in H. Schultze, *Kleine deutsche Geschichte*, Munich 1996, 198, exhibited in the Deutsches Historisches Museum in Berlin. The representative of economic reason quoted is the Nobel prize winner F.A. Hayek (1899–1992) in a lecture given on 6 February 1979 to Freiburg University (according to *Die Zeit*, no. 37, September 1997, 37f.). The peace prize winner of the German book trade and Nobel prize winner who along with his wife argued for com-pulsory sterilization was Gunnar Myrdal, who with Alva Myrdal wrote a book *Kris I befolkningsfrågan* in 1934. He became very well known through his works against racism, poverty and under-development. The sermon refers to the death of Princess Diana on 31 August 1997. Her funeral had been broadcast for hours on television on the day before the sermon.

Honest Zacchaeus

A plea for the rehabilitation of a senior tax collector

(Luke 19.1–10)

He entered Jericho and was passing through the city. A man named Zacchaeus lived there; he was the chief tax collector, and very rich. He very much wanted to see who this Jesus was, but the crowd blocked his view, because he was short. So he ran on ahead and climbed up into a sycamore tree to see him, for he was to pass that way. When Jesus came to the place, he looked up and said to him, 'Zaccheus, come down quickly; for I must stay at your house today.' So he came down quickly, and received him joyfully. When they saw it the crowd were indignant and said, 'He has gone to be the guest of a man who is a sinner.' And Zaccheus turned to the Lord and said, 'Behold, Lord, half of my possessions I give to the poor; and if I have asked too much of any one, I will give it back fourfold.' And Jesus said to him, 'Today salvation has been given to this house, since this man is also a son of Abraham. For the Son of man came to seek and to save the lost.'

The story of Zaccheus begins with the sentence:

He entered Jericho and was passing through the city.

How good it would be if one simply had to vary this sentence a little: and he entered Heidelberg and was passing through the city; he, Jesus, the hiding place of the invisible God, a bit of transcendence to grasp. It would be good if one could at least say that he comes in his message to us. But this message is like many letters at the present time. We hear, 'A letter has been sent to you, addressed to you, on an important matter.' But it doesn't come. The postal strike is not only between Berlin and Munich but between heaven and earth. Perhaps the letter to you was lost long ago. Perhaps it will still reach you. Or perhaps never.

You wait for this letter like the underling in Kafka's parable of the imperial embassage. The emperor sent news to you, his wretched underling, on his death-bed. The messenger is on the way. But one obstacle after another crops up. He finds it difficult to make his way through the crowd. He has to get over one palace wall after another. The message will never arrive. And what do you do? The parable ends with the words, 'But you sit at your window and dream of it when evening comes.'

It was all simpler in Jericho at that time. There too there was someone dreaming that the message would come. He was some-one who could not see Jesus, a blind beggar. He had only heard that Jesus was on his way. He crouched there, in front of the city. He got to Jesus over all the obstacles. And Jesus healed him so that he could see. And he too was following Jesus when he entered the city.

The next sentence in our story says of this city:

> A man named Zacchaeus lived there; he was the chief tax col-
> lector, and very rich.

The evangelist Luke has put the two inhabitants of Jericho side by side: the beggar, right down at the bottom of the local hier-archy, and the chief tax collector, right at the top. He has deliberately made a literary link between these people, who in reality had always lived side by side with no link whatsoever. And how is it today? If the message should reach you one day, if it doesn't get completely lost on the way, you may be certain that it will connect you with people whom you have previously passed by. At that time a beggar and a chief tax collector were brought together. Today the equivalent might be a street person and the head of the Treasury.

But there is more in this contrast between the two. Just imagine all the people living on earth divided into five groups of equal size. And the wealth of the whole world has been piled up opposite them, divided into five equal portions. The first group of people, which includes us, possesses four of these portions (indeed rather more). But the other four groups have to be content with one portion. In the sobering figures of the 1993 United Nations Development Programme, that means that the first 20% of the world population possesses 82.7% of the world's income. The last 20% possesses only 1.4%. That is the relationship between the beggar and the chief tax collector today.

Perhaps you will find the message which is on its way to you somewhat uncanny. Perhaps you're now sitting at your window and dreaming that it may go past you. For it will hurt you, bring you grief, and make you perplexed.

But let's read on:

> He very much wanted to see who this Jesus was, but the crowd blocked his view, because he was short. So he ran on ahead and climbed up into a sycamore tree to see him, for he was to pass that way.

Zacchaeus didn't stay sitting at the window, dreaming of the message. He went into action. Because he was small, he had to get away from the crowd. So he climbed a tree – rather beneath the dignity of the chief tax collector! Isn't it just the same with us today? This message which is on the way to you will require you to become active. Don't say, 'I'm a few sizes too small for it. I'm no athlete and climber in social ethics. I'm tone deaf to religion, like most of my contemporaries.' All these thoughts will keep you hidden in the vast crowd. If you want to hear the message, break away from the crowd. Go your own way. If you do, you will have to go against the trend, and of course you'll be criticized.

It's the same with Zacchaeus. Let's continue:

> When Jesus came to the place, he looked up and said to him, 'Zacchaeus, come down quickly; for I must stay at your

house today. So he came down quickly, and received him joyfully. When they saw it the crowd were indignant and said,
'He has gone to be the guest of a man who is a sinner.'

Jesus and Zacchaeus: they don't go together any better than fire
and water. The one preaches that one should lend money without asking for it back. The other lives on extracting money from
other people, even using methods which are criminal. Isn't
Zacchaeus one of those people who understand doctored
balance sheets, vanished credits, false bankruptcies?

Many of you will say, 'This message isn't addressed to me.
I'm no crooked businessman or fraudulent company director.'
But let's read on.

And Zacchaeus turned to the Lord and said, 'Behold, Lord,
half of my possessions I give to the poor; and if have asked
too much of any one, I will give it back fourfold.'

You can understand the mail between heaven and earth going
on strike over this message. How is it to be delivered? Give
away half your possessions? Make good fourfold for any cheating? What have we to do with Zacchaeus?

I want to suggest two reflections on this message. The first is
that Zacchaeus isn't a notoriously criminal businessman, but
has an average business morality, of the kind that is customary
today. Here I must do a little calculation. What strikes me is
that Zacchaeus is certain that he has earned half his possessions
honestly. For he doesn't explain giving away this half as something that he has to make good. Nor has the other half in any
way simply been earned dishonestly. For Zacchaeus must be
certain that he doesn't need to spent all the 50% that he has left
for purposes of reparation. After all, he has to live. And in addition there is hospitality for Jesus, including his followers: the
twelve disciples, a beggar from Jericho and many others. If we
assume at least 10% for this purpose, then we are still left with
40% for reparations. Now Zacchaeus wants to repay fourfold
any money that he has earned by cheating. The conclusion must

be that Zacchaeus assumes that at most 10% of his possessions, but probably much less, has been obtained crookedly.

So we can hardly brand him a great sinner. In my view, the crowd's criticism is sheer hypocrisy. And it would also be hypocrisy today, in a country in which withholding tax evasion and cheating on insurance contributions have become a mark of cleverness, and moonlighting a popular sport. Who can really swear that, say, 10% of his or her income hasn't been earned outside the law? Zacchaeus is one of us. Comparisons with the fraudsters who make the headlines are misleading and only distractions. The message has the right address on it. We are Zacchaeus. And if we aren't Zacchaeus yet, we shall become Zacchaeus later. I'm aware that there are many people at this service who have so far never filled in a tax return and may display an enviable moralism on these questions. But for how long?

So the address is correct. But isn't the content of the message exaggerated? It would be unworldly here to propagate giving away half one's possessions and an x% reparations tax. The rabbis of the New Testament period were more realistic. For church tax, giving and charitable work they required at least 2–3% of annual income; at most one might give away 20%. Those are realistic figures.

Yet I can also get something out of Zacchaeus's figures. And that is my second consideration. Let's look again at the world-wide distribution of possessions. A fifth of the world population has four-fifths of the world's resources. We belong to this privileged fifth. If we had half as much, we would still have 40%. In the world-wide distribution of income we would then approach conditions which would be comparable to those in the Federal Republic – and even then they are worryingly asymmetrical, above all because they are becoming more so year by year. That can't be good in the long run.

And what about reparations? World-wide they are impossible. Too much indicates that our wealth as a whole is the result of an unfair system. So far the world market has functioned in such a way that the poor countries are becoming increasingly poor and the rich countries are becoming increasingly rich. Something is fundamentally wrong here. In my view it's deceit not to concede that, although we profit from it all.

I can't offer a solution here, nor is that my task. It isn't even reprehensible not to know a solution. It's reprehensible only to deny the problem, not to perceive the great challenge of the present and the future. I would define it like this. The important thing is to construct a social market economy world-wide which is compatible with our natural resources, a social market economy which one hopes is more social than it is with us. For this purpose we must probably do a good deal of rethinking and make changes at many points. We must do that simply in our own long-term interest, so that we can live on this small planet in peace with one another and with nature. That's a hard demand – and a great challenge. It's part of the message today. But the message includes even more. It doesn't just consist of a demand and a command.

The text continues with the words:

> And Jesus said to him, 'Today salvation has been given to this house, since this man is also a son of Abraham.'

Jesus doesn't say, 'Today Zacchaeus has experienced salvation because he has converted, because from now on he means to use his possessions for the benefit of society.' He defends Zacchaeus against the criticism of the crowd with another argument. What is decisive for him isn't what Zacchaeus has done or wants to do, but his being. He is a child of Abraham. He has the same status as all his critics. And no one can deprive him of this status.

There also is the message to you: God's call assigns you a status which no one can take from you – and which doesn't depend on how good or how bad your behaviour is. Nor does it depend on how successful or how unsuccessful your life has been so far. Certainly we aren't children of Abraham by birth. But we become so by a new birth when God's word recreates us.

Then we belong to the eternal covenant of God with his children. Then the promise 'Today salvation has come to us' applies to us.

Salvation isn't a promise for a world in the beyond. For already *today*, when you hear the message and it comes to you, already *today* the beyond is breaking into your life.

Already today, if you accept Jesus into your heart, the morning radiance of eternity will shine out in him. Nothing in the future can surpass what happens at the moment when God enters your life and makes it infinitely valuable.

How often have you sat at the window in the evening and dreamed that the message might come? *Today* it can reach you: it can reach you any day, as long as that means '*today*' for you. And then this moment will become a bit of eternity – in the midst of time.

The last sentence of our text sums up this message:

For the Son of man came to seek and to save the lost.

This message has already been on the way to you for a long time. Long before you were born, it was meant for you and all men and women. Think how many days you've been waiting for it. You were worried that the letter might perhaps have got lost. You were annoyed because the post between heaven and earth was functioning so badly, and the postmen were on strike. Moreover, postmen are often very problematical. Nevertheless, you got the message today. And what do you read, what do you hear, when you open the letter?

You read that it wasn't the letter that got lost in this world. It was you.

You read that the letter that you expected will never come. Because you are the letter. You yourself are the letter that got lost. You yourself are the messenger who has to fight through obstacles to reach your destination.

That is the message: you are a thought of God with which God wants to enrich his creation. You are a message for your

143

parents, for your friends, for your fellow men and women, for everyone. But you didn't know. You didn't want to see what a valuable message your life contains. Information is contained in you which doesn't exist anywhere else.

You were lost, because you simply kept sitting by the window, waiting for the great message. But others had been waiting a long time for you.

You were lost because you kept asking, 'How can the others help me? How can they benefit me?' But you yourself are someone who can help and benefit.

You were lost because you thought that you were too small for the greatest thing that a person can experience between cradle and grave: God coming into a life and changing it.

You yourself are the lost letter. It is addressed to others. Others have long been sitting by the window dreaming that you would come – and bring light into their lives.

Others are waiting for you to do something with them so that the street people don't perish.

Others are waiting for you to indicate their discontent that a fifth of humankind has four-fifths of all resources.

Others are waiting for you to work with them so that we don't choke on our own products.

Others are waiting for you to support them with a small gift – or for you once in your life to make a larger bequest. (I would also recommend that to Zacchaeus, instead of simply giving away all his possessions.)

Others are waiting for you – perhaps only to visit them or to telephone them, or to give them a friendly smile.

But perhaps you rightly say, 'I'm only a weak, vulnerable person.' Perhaps things are going so badly with you that you don't even feel strong enough to become a message. Perhaps you're sick and don't have long to live. Nevertheless, you're a message from God to this world – with all your limitations and vulnerability. Jesus too was limited and vulnerable. He too didn't live long. Yet he was the hiding-place of the invisible God, a bit of transcendence in this world. Allow yourself to be changed by him, so that you are utterly certain that you too are a good idea of God's. You too are a message of life to us all. God also wants to say something, to express something, through your life. God also wants to use you to increase his peace.

And may the peace of God which surpasses all our understanding keep your hearts and minds in Christ Jesus. Amen.

This sermon was given in St Peter's Church, Heidelberg, on 26 June 1994. I have taken the information about the distribution of possessions on our earth from U. Duchrow, *Alternativen zur kapitalistischen Weltwirtschaft. Biblische Erinnerung und politische Ansätze zur Überwindung einer lebensbedrohenden Ökonomie*, Gütersloh and Mainz 1994. The sermon alludes to warning token strikes in June 1994: in that period it was impossible to calculate whether and when a letter had reached its addressee. Various scandals were being discussed in the media at that time. The furniture dealer J. Schneider and the gymnasium floor manufacturer Balsam had falsely declared bankruptcy; Schneider had fled abroad to escape his billions of DM debts. The managing director of Balsam had been imprisoned. At the same time there was discussion of the business practices of the Munich Christian Socialist leader Peter Gauweiler, who while still minister had 'leased' out the clients of his legal practice for DM 10,000 a month; this inevitably aroused the suspicion that as a minister he would get lucrative commissions from this practice.

I Am Who I Am

A sign of life in life

(John 1.19–23)

> *And this is the testimony of John, when the Jews sent priests and Levites from Jerusalem to ask him, 'Who are you?' He confessed, he did not deny, but confessed, 'I am not the Christ.' And they asked him, 'What then? Are you Elijah?' He said, 'I am not.' 'Are you the prophet?' And he answered, 'No.' They said to him then, 'Who are you? Let us have an answer for those who sent us. What do you say about yourself?' He said, 'I am the voice of one crying in the wilderness, "Make straight the way of the Lord," as the prophet Isaiah said.'*

'This is a testimony.' That's how our text begins. This introduction suggests that someone is on trial – for a crime. In fact these are the most remarkable proceedings in the world, proceedings in which someone is himself and stands there – and refuses to be what others expect of him.

'This is the testimony of John, when the Jews sent priests and Levites from Jerusalem to ask him, "Who are you?"'

John the Baptist is on trial. He is the first Christian. Some would dispute that he is a Christian. Some would say that at best he is a Christian in waiting, a potential Christian. All the more reason for us to identify with him. There are many among us who understand ourselves as Christians in waiting, many who at any rate are provisional Christians. There are many who would be happy if at least they could say that honestly. Furthermore, in Advent all Christians are again Christians in waiting. In Advent the question arises anew for everyone: 'Who are you? Who are we?'

Who puts this question? Before which tribunal is it discussed? The text speaks of priests and Levites. At that time they were the administrators of the holy. They established the frontiers between salvation and damnation, health and sickness, good and evil. John the Baptist is interrogated by them. They ask him, 'Who are you?' The question is put three times. Three times he gives answers which perhaps are helpful for Christians in Advent.

The first question runs: 'Who are you?' Of John the Baptist's reply it is said: 'He confessed, he did not deny, but confessed, "I am not the Christ." ' This answer doesn't match the question. No one had asked him, 'Are you the Christ? Are you the one who brings salvation?' This jump between question and answer will occupy us later. First, it may be sufficient to point out that John has detected the real question between the words. Don't we all know it? The question whether we really are Christians is often put to us indirectly – as a question about our opinion about this or that, concealed in general talk about identity and faith. Sometimes we don't even notice that we are being tested to see whether we are Christians. Every year we keep having the experience of 'priests' with a friendly smile sitting around and wanting to read the riot act. Their unspoken question is, 'Are you a Christian? Confess it and don't deny it. Basically you're not a Christian. At most you're a Christian in waiting. And now you're being put to the test. Now you're being weighed and found too light.'

Those who escape the theologians are interrogated by other tribunals: by the great advocates of meaning in our society – by psychotherapists, sociologists, journalists and of course also philosophers. They all ask us, 'Who are you? What have you made of yourself? Have you become what you really are? Tell us. Confess and don't deny it.' The apostles of the culture of self-realization can read one the riot act just as much as the apostles of a traditional kind. John the Baptist's answer is a help before all such tribunals. For none of us knows who we really are. We all know for certain only what we aren't. We can certainly say with John, 'I am not the Christ. I am not the light of the world. I am not the way, the truth and the life. At best

I'm a small light, at best a detour, perhaps even a wrong turning.' Human identity consists in what we aren't. Hence the truth of the maxim, 'Tell me who you aren't, and I can guess who you could be.' But even then no one knows. Even then we don't know.

Now for John's second answer: 'And they asked him, "What then? Are you Elijah?" He said, "I am not." ' The question is: if you aren't already bringing salvation, are you at least someone who is fighting damnation, who kills the priests of Baal and keeps the powerful in the world aware of their injustice? A zealot for good and against evil? The Christians and Jews of the first century regarded John the Baptist as Elijah. Why doesn't he rise to these expectations? Why does he deny being Elijah? People would immediately have accepted that from him. I find his 'no' sympathetic. We know that some zeal for the faith is rooted in an attempt to foist one's own identity problems on others. One takes the side of the priests and Levites. In that case one doesn't have to ask oneself, 'Who am I? Am I a Christian? Am I a non-Christian?' It is far simpler to perplex others with such questions than to endure one's own perplexities. That is what I mean when I say that some people foist their identity problems on others. Dogmatic rigidity, moralizing zeal for faith, not being able to accept people with an open identity – all that can be an indication here.

I notice something of this in myself, too, when the wrath of Elijah comes upon me. It happened recently, when in a small neighbouring country, on the day of national celebration, I saw a national flag lying on the altar – and the Bible on this flag. I was alone in the church. For a moment I wanted to tear the flag from the altar. Isn't someone who accords the national symbol the same place in a church as the Bible a priest of Baal, one who confuses God and the idols? I didn't tear the flag from the altar. I didn't want headlines in the newspaper: 'German Professor of Theology Desecrates Church.' Of course I firmly believe that no national flag belongs on an altar. Here, in St Peter's Church, I would tear it down. But had I torn it down then, commentaries could have appeared in the country's newspaper to the effect that here a German intellectual had projected his ambivalent attitude to his nationality on to others. The understandable anger against the errors of German nationalism (and national Protestantism) was being turned into aggression against the more harmless nationalism of other peoples. And that wouldn't be wholly wrong.

So we are to learn from John the Baptist's answer: don't react to the question 'Who are you?' with the wrath of Elijah. Don't mask the perplexity which the question causes you with zeal against others.

Let's listen to John's third answer. When asked, 'Are you the prophet?', he answers, 'No.' The question says: 'If you aren't bringing salvation as Christ or destroying disaster like Elijah, then do you at least have a vision of future salvation or of the future overcoming of evil? Are you at least a prophet?' Anyone who is uncertainty of his identity dreams of the future. That is often the only way in which people living in repressive conditions can remain true to themselves. But those who live in freedom can also avoid the question 'Who are you?' by dreams of the future. We all know the kind of person who says, 'From now on everything is going to be different.' We know this kind of person so well because such a person lives in each of us. When he was young he said, 'When I grow up, everything is going to be different.' When he studied, he said, 'When I pass the examination, everything is going to be different.' When he sent off the first job applications, he said, 'When I get a safe job, everything is going to be different.' When he got a safe job, he said, 'When I've built a house, everything is going to be different.' And when he had settled down he said, 'When I retire, everything is going to be be different.' And then everything was different. After retirement came death. And then everything was quite different from what he had expected. It became very quiet. And the bells tolled. And he was put in the grave. And if one thinks about it, things can get very different.

So don't let us play the prophet with our own lives when we

are to answer the question 'Who are you?' Certainly prophets and dreams are a great productive force – in the life of the individual and in society. With them we reassure ourselves of the standards of a better life. But the radicalism of some utopias has already kept some people from radically necessary insights into reality. So like John the Baptist we shouldn't react to the question 'Who are you?' as prophets. Don't let's say what we shall become or what we could be or what we dream of being one day.

But what should we say? Let's read the conclusion of our text. 'They said to him then, "Who are you? Let us have an answer for those who sent us. What do you say about yourself?" He said, "I am the voice of one crying in the wilderness, 'Make straight the way of the Lord,' as the prophet Isaiah said." '

First, John says, 'I am the voice of one crying in the wilderness. I break the silence of the wilderness. I bear witness to light where there is darkness. I call for life where death rules.' He is utterly caught up in this activity. That is what he is. From this we can learn that being a Christian is a call to life and light. And like John we ourselves cannot give light, but only bear witness to the light that we already find there. Like John we shouldn't identify ourselves with the roles which are assigned to us. How easy it would have been for him to say, 'I'm a prophet.' 'I'm Elijah.' That would have been accepted. That accorded with his image. When we ask ourselves, 'Who are we?', we can't refer to such standardized roles. Don't let's say, 'We're baptized and Protestant, examined and ordained, habilitated or rehabilitated.' None of that counts. Everyone is more than any role. Everyone longs to be more. At all events, when asked who you are, you can say, 'I'm a call to life. I'm a longing for light.'

Secondly, John replies with the invitation, 'Prepare the way of the Lord.' He doesn't say, 'I am the way,' or even 'I am the one who prepares the way for the Lord.' Although he is asked about himself and only about himself, he replies with an appeal to all. He looks for others who will prepare the way of the Lord with him, to cut a path in life, to bear witness to the light. He can't do that alone. No one can. The world is dark and cold. But where people together resist its darkness and cold, where together they set out and do not disparage themselves in an inquisitorial way – a light dawns. When asked, 'Who are you?', reply, 'I'm someone in search of other people who will go along the way with me.'

Thirdly, John the Baptist refers to the prophet Isaiah. He takes up an age-old tradition. The Gospel of John says that in the vision at his call in the temple Isaiah did not see God, but Jesus. The Gospel of John emphasizes that no one has ever seen God; God is visible only in Jesus. And it concludes from this that wherever God encounters men and women (as in the many encounters with God in the Old Testament), Jesus is really there. Let's learn from this that we Christians aren't the first to have experiences of God. Let's trust the Gospel of John here: where God is experienced authentically, the same light, the same life, the same will is manifested as in Jesus. So when asked, 'Who are you?', say, 'I'm someone who fits in the long history of those who ask about God, who set out on the way to him' – together with Jews, Muslims and many others.

Can we now say before the tribunals of the world who we are? Do we know? Hasn't it all got even more enigmatic? More open? More difficult? So let's go back to the first question put to John the Baptist, 'Who are you?,' and to the answer, 'I am not the Christ.' There is a jump between question and answer. But could there be a deeper significance behind this jump? Doesn't John the Baptist mean, 'Only if I were Christ could I say who I am?' And isn't he right? In the Gospel of John, isn't Christ the only one who can authentically say, 'I AM?' He says it often in connection with images. He says. 'I AM the bread of life. I AM the light of the world. I AM the good shepherd. I AM the door. I AM the way. I AM the vine.' Each time, with these images Jesus says, 'I am more than others seek and see in me.' People seek the Christ, the Prophet, the Son of God in him. But in the end Jesus reveals what he is in images of himself. However, he also says his I AM without any image, with no predicate or addition. He reveals himself as the absolute I AM, just as elsewhere in the Bible only God reveals himself as the one who can say, 'I AM WHO I AM. I WILL BE WHO I WILL BE.'

Away from this God, any human being can only say, 'I am not who I really am. I am far from myself.' But close to this God, anyone may hope to be able to say 'I am'. In the Gospel of John Jesus is the first person to say 'I AM'. And he wants all people to be able to say it as he does, although they are far from God and far from themselves.

He promises that he and the Father will leave their heavenly dwellings to take up their abode with us. God does not will to dwell only in Jesus; God wills to dwell in all.

God, who alone can say I AM, will be in you, so that you too can say I AM. God, who is far from you, wills to be light and life in you.

So don't say that tomorrow everything will be different. God wants to fulfil your life today – God wants to be true life in you so that it seems to you as if previously you had only existed inauthentically, like a shadow, like a question, like a longing.

Don't say, 'In any case, my life is worthless. It's ruined.' If God enters your life, then it will be filled with the highest value. Your life cannot be more valuable, become more valuable.

Don't say, 'Tomorrow it will all be over', because the shadow of death has fallen on your life and you have to depart – earlier than others. That is bitter. But if God takes up his abode in you, then eternity has touched you.

So prepare the way for him! Above all prepare the way to yourself! Open the door of your life! Take down the bolts and bars with which you protect yourself against his coming! Let God in to you! God wants to urge you through Jesus to be yourself. He wants to urge you to the most remarkable action in the world, to stand up for yourself and no longer to be just what others expect of you. For you are worth infinitely more than others say and think of you.

Wherever you can say, 'I am really alive', a breath of the one who alone is real has touched you. Wherever you can say, 'I've found myself,' God has found you. Wherever God's presence embraces you, you can say I AM. And wherever you can say 'I AM WHO I AM', you have become an image of the one who defined himself as 'I AM WHO I AM. I WILL BE WHO I WILL BE.'

And may the peace of God which surpasses all our understanding keep your hearts and minds in Christ Jesus. Amen.

This sermon was given in St Peter's Church, Heidelberg, on 18 December 1994. Germany's sympathetic small neighbour, where I saw the national flag lying on the altar on the day of national celebration, is Switzerland.

Is Christian Faith Necessarily Intolerant?

A sermon on the first article of the Theological Declaration of Barmen

(John 14.6)

'I am the way, and the truth, and the life; no one comes to the Father, but by me' (John 14.6).

'Truly, truly, I say to you, I am the door of the sheep. All who came before me are thieves and robbers . . . I am the door; if anyone enters by me, he will be saved' (John 10.7–9).

'Jesus Christ, as he is testified to us in Holy Scripture, is the one Word of God, whom we are to hear, whom we are to trust and obey in life and death.

We repudiate the false teaching that the church can and must recognize yet other happenings and powers, figures and truths as divine revelation alongside this one word of God, as a source of her preaching' (Barmen Theological Declaration, first thesis).

'I am the way, and the truth, and the life' – these words of Jesus radiate a great warmth when one is in a hopeless situation, when no way can be seen by which life can go on, when a voice says to us, 'It's all in vain.' Then they are a marvellous counter to our desperation: 'But there is a way. There is life. There is true life. There is a way to God.'

However, there's another statement after these words which seems to many people to be harsh and cold. 'I am the way, and the truth, and the life; no one comes to the Father, but by me.' Doesn't that cut many people off from God? Do our Muslim fellow citizens, who pray in around 700 mosques in Germany, have no access to God? And what about the Jews? They still need a way to the Father, since they were already his children. They revealed to us the way to the one and only God – we didn't do it. And what about our friends who have become alienated from Christianity and nevertheless are good people? Can we still speak as harshly today as Jesus in the Gospel of John? Isn't that intolerant?

Only in one instance may one be intolerant; only in one instance may one speak in an intolerant way. One must be intolerant of intolerance. I want to demonstrate that by means of two situations.

The first situation takes us back sixty years, to the second year after Hitler seized power. At that time the resistance against Hitler formed in the church under this saying: 'I am the way, and the truth, and the life; no one comes to the Father, but by me.' It was the introduction to the first thesis of the Barmen Theological Declaration of 1934 – the beginning of a turning away of Protestantism from a terrible false course, a false course which had begun long before Hitler.

The wars of liberation against Napoleon at the beginning of the last century were already experienced by many as a religious revival. After that, Protestants increasingly identified the cause of their nation with God's cause. When in 1870 the Germans were victorious at Sedan in a baneful war against France, Kaiser Wilhelm remarked, 'What a turning point through God's providence!' When the young soldiers went to war in the First World War, the words 'God with Us' were stamped on the buckles of their belts. Many saw the rise of Germany to become a great power as the will of God. For them, God revealed himself in the national destiny. Protestantism became national Protestantism, and for this national Protestantism it was unbelievable that the Germans could have lost the First World War. How could God have allowed such a thing? That could only be a test on the way to a yet more powerful, yet more famous, yet stronger Germany.

Therefore most Protestants experienced the time of the Weimar Republic – with weak governments and economic crises – as a humiliation. They longed for a strong government which would restore the damaged self-confidence of the Germans. So the incomprehensible happened to us: the vast majority of Protestant Christians (already at that time it was estimated at around eighty per cent) welcomed Hitler's seizure of power. Many saw the finger of God in it. At that time one of the leading theologians, a university professor, remarked: if in times of crisis and need the 'destiny of our people to a true and worthy life' is realized by a leader, 'then in truth we have heard more than a human voice'. Here Hitler had become the one who led the people to truth and to life. His voice was the voice of God. He was salvation. Hence the greeting 'Heil Hitler!'.

I have to confess that when I read something like this I am overcome by anger, fury and shame. My consolation is that even at that time there were Christians who were seized with anger at such statements. And more than that; they did something about it.

Hitler wanted to bring the churches into line, i.e. make them an instrument of his criminal policy. He concluded a concordat with the Catholic church, made promises which he then did not keep. In return, the political representatives of Catholicism probably assented to that enabling law which made Hitler dictator. The Catholic church people, who were much more clearly against Hitler than most Protestants, were betrayed at that time by their church leaders. Hitler played the hierarchy off against the Catholics. With the Protestants he chose another strategy. Here he mobilized the church people against the church governments. He forced all Protestants to take part in the church elections and to elect his adherents, the so-called 'German Christians'. Thus people who otherwise never went to church and were not at all interested in it, suddenly created new majorities in church governments and synods. The old church governments were deposed, with three exceptions: in Hanover, Württemberg and Bavaria the churches remained intact.

What did the National Socialist Christians want? One important point in their programme was the dismissal of all pastors of Jewish descent and a refusal to admit Jews to the church. The resistance formed against this. At that time there were around 18,000 pastors in Germany, 4,000 of whom declared that they could never accept the dismissal of pastors of Jewish descent. Others joined their number later. This was the hour of the birth of the Confessing Church – a counter-church to the official church, which almost everywhere was dominated by the Nazis. This counter-church organized free synods. At the first great Confessing Synod in Barmen a declaration was passed which in its first thesis got to the roots of the basic evil. Against the thesis that Hitler was the way to the truth and life, it set the two sayings from the Gospel of John.

Jesus Christ says: 'I am the way, and the truth, and the life; no one comes to the Father, but by me.' And it added: 'Truly, truly, I say to you, I am the door of the sheep. All who came before me are thieves and robbers . . . I am the door; if anyone enters by me, he will be saved.'

Just think: here, with a combination of quotations from the Bible, it is said that if Hitler claims to show salvation, then he is a thief and a murderer. Anyone with ears to hear certainly understood that at the time.

But why had Hitler been able to become the voice of God for so many Protestants? Why did they seek salvation in him? Because for them, nationalism was the highest God. Because their belief was 'Deutschland, Deutschland über alles', Germany over all. They believed that anyone who exalted this nation above all other nations had a commission from God. They recognized other voices as the voice of God alongside the gospel, alongside the voice of Jesus, alongside the Bible. The Barmen Declaration speaks out against this. Tersely and clearly it says: 'We repudiate the false teaching that the church can and must recognize yet other happenings and powers, figures and truths as divine revelation alongside this one word of God, as a source of her preaching.' What kind of other happenings were these? They were the wars in which Germany had been victorious. And what other powers were these? They were the nation and the state which for many people was the voice of God in the form of the law. What other figures? They were figures like Hitler! And what other truths? The National Socialist world view which said that what served nation and race was true. Against all this it is said:

'Jesus Christ, as he is testified to us in Holy Scripture, is the one Word of God, whom we are to hear, whom we are to trust and obey in life and death.' Him and no other.

Of course all that is now in the past. But it can happen again at any time. Some politicians are already wondering whether the nation doesn't have a religious value. Whether national ties shouldn't replace the tie to Christianity which is slackening. I think that that is a mistake and should have no chance among us. And at the moment it has no chance.

Another problem is more important. And that brings us to the second situation in which intolerance against intolerance is required. Many people are now saying that the abrupt denial of any revelation outside Jesus may have been necessary and relevant at that time, but today it is obsolete. The correct insight here is that the theologian who was crucial in formulating the Barmen Declaration, Karl Barth, later toned down his judgment. He accepted that God has made lights shine everywhere in creation. The light is not bright in Christ alone. But here God's light shines clearly, so that we can measure all lights by his light. For me, that means that I am convinced that people of other faiths, Jews, Muslims, Hindus, Buddhists and others, have authentic experiences of God. But I cannot imagine myself accepting anything as the voice of God which contradicts the way of Jesus, his life, his truth. That is the way in which the Barmen Theological Declaration is understood almost universally today. It doesn't say that God doesn't reveal himself anywhere in the world apart from Jesus. But it does say that the church doesn't make that the foundation of its proclamation. Its foundation is the revelation in Jesus. By this it must measure and examine everything. He, Jesus, is the touchstone for everything.

Now sceptics could ask, 'How can Jesus be a touchstone when the way to him is itself so full of stones? Hasn't Jesus disappeared behind age-old texts, behind a long church history with much in it that is pernicious, covered over in a church which often presents his word in a most unconvincing way? Where is the Jesus to be found who is to be the way, the truth and the life?' Jesus himself gives an answer to this in the New Testament. He says:

> I was hungry and you gave me no food,
> I was thirsty and you gave me no drink,
> I was a stranger
> and you did not welcome me,
> I was naked and you did not clothe me,
> I was sick and in prison
> and you did not visit me.

And then we will ask him, 'Where did you meet us?' And he will tell us:

> 'As you did it to one of the least of these my brethren, you did it to me.'

And here again the harsh statement by Jesus applies: 'No one comes to the Father but by me.' No one comes to the Father who has failed to hear the voice of Jesus in the least of his sisters and brothers. And that applies to all of them: to Christians, Jews, Muslims, Hindus and Buddhists. Jesus encounters all human beings incognito in those who need help. There he reveals himself. There he opens the way to the Father for us. There he shines out as the light that lightens everyone coming into the world, as we are told at the beginning of the Gospel of John. There we hear his voice.

But that means that we do not hear his voice in the history of the nation and the state, as the German Christians thought. Rather, we hear it in those who are the victims of nationalism and state power. Anyone who fails to hear these voices of the victims, of the sick, of the imprisoned, of the aliens, and who does not recognize aliens as sisters and brothers – will not get to the Father. That sounds intolerant. But that is intolerance against intolerance. Here is an illustration of how necessary such intolerance is.

> A coloured asylum-seeker wanted to be accepted into a white church. The pastor had his reservations. 'I'm not sure whether that would be fair on our church members. I suggest that you go home and pray and wait to see what God has to say to you about it.' Some days later the asylum-seeker returned. 'Pastor,' he said, 'I've followed your advice. I spoke to God about the matter and he said to me, "Remember that you're dealing with a very exclusive church. You probably won't get in. I myself have been trying for many years, but so far I haven't succeeded."'

What does that mean? It means that a church which shuts its doors on the oppressed is no longer God's church. Because some Christians recognized that sixty years ago and insisted on accepting Jews into their church and giving them the same rights as all other members of the congregation, they formed a counter-church to the official churches. Unfortunately it must also be said that even this counter-church, even the Confessing Church, kept silent far too long about the injustice being done to Jews, and there was no word on their behalf in the Barmen Theological Declaration, no statement that Jesus too was a Jew, not even a mention that the Old Testament, the Bible of the Jews, is also our Bible. Some people already made this criticism at the time. They had partial success: in 1936 the Confessing Church published a protest against the persecution of the Jews, against the concentration camps, against the contempt for the law.

A church which stands in the succession of the Confessing Church is warned: we must make sure that we don't protest too late, react too slowly, when people are discriminated against. We would have no excuse. We will not be persecuted if we stand up for aliens and asylum-seekers. We will even be applauded by many if in well-founded cases congregations grant church asylum, i.e. hinder a planned deportation, in order to support people in danger. A church which counts the Barmen Theological Declaration among its foundations cannot do otherwise. For it, the saying of Jesus, 'I am the way, and the truth, and the life; no one comes to the Father, but by me', remains the guideline. And that means that no one comes to the Father except by the way of solidarity which Jesus has shown.

That applies both to the church and to each individual among us. I know that at every service there are people for whom life is shrouded in darkness. Some perhaps find it difficult to listen because their head is so full of their own anxieties. To them I want to say, 'Even if a sad voice in you says, "There is no way, no truth, no life," there is still a loud counter-voice: "I am the way, the truth, and the life." There is a voice which says, "Despite everything there is a way. There is life. There is true life."' Only because individual Christians keep experiencing that in dark hours in their personal lives does the church as a whole also have the power to follow the truth in the dark hours of history – then in Barmen and, I hope, also in the present and the future.

And may the peace of God which surpasses all our understanding keep your hearts and minds in Christ Jesus. Amen.

This sermon was preached in Reichelsheim in the Odenwald on 18 September 1994, in a series of sermons on the Barmen Theological Declaration. The university theologian quoted in the sermon is P. Althaus, *Die deutsche Stunde der Kirche*, Göttingen ²1934, 12: 'And if the destiny of our people to true and worthy life at a time of madness and forgetfulness again becomes the law for many through the call of a leader, then in truth they have heard more than the voice of a man.' Quoted from B. Hamm, 'Schuld und Verstrickung der Kirche. Vorüberlegungen zu einer Darstellung der Erlanger Theologie in der Zeit des Nationalsozialismus', in W.Stegemann (ed.), *Kirche und Nationalsozialismus*, Stuttgart 1990, 13–49: 14 n. 1. The story of the coloured asylum-seeker is a variation on H.L. Gee, 'Wer einer dieser Geringsten ausschliesst', in L. Graf, U. Kabitz, M. Lienhard and R. Pertsch, *Die Blumen des Blinden*, Munich 1983, 157.

The Weaker Members as the Strength of the Body of Christ

A sign of life from the Holy Spirit

(I Corinthians 12.12–31)

For just as the body is one and has many members, and all the members of the body, though many, are one body, so it is with Christ. For by one Spirit we were all baptized into one body – Jews or Greeks, slaves or free – and all were made to drink of one Spirit. For the body does not consist of one member but of many. If the foot should say, 'Because I am not a hand, I do not belong to the body,' that would not make it any less a part of the body. And if the ear should say, 'Because I am not an eye, I do not belong to the body,' that would not make it any less a part of the body. If the whole body were an eye, where would be the hearing? If the whole body were an ear, where would be the sense of smell? But as it is, God arranged the organs in the body, each one of them, as he chose. If all were a single organ, where would the body be? As it is, there are many parts, yet one body. The eye cannot say to the hand, 'I have no need of you,' nor again the head to the feet, 'I have no need of you.' On the contrary, the parts of the body which seem to be weaker are indispensable, and those parts of the body which we think less honourable we invest with the greater honour, and our unpresentable parts are treated with greater modesty, which our more presentable parts do not require. But God has so composed the body, giving the greater honour to the inferior part, that there may be no discord in the body, but that the members may have the same care for one another. If one member suffers, all suffer together; if one member is honoured, all rejoice together. Now you are the body of Christ and individually members of it. And God has appointed in the church first apostles, second prophets, third teachers, then workers of miracles, then healers, helpers, administrators, speakers in various kinds of tongues. Are all apostles? Are all prophets? Are all teachers? Do all work miracles? Do all possess gifts of healing? Do all speak with tongues? Do all interpret? But

earnestly desire the higher gifts. And I will show you a still more
excellent way.

We are the body of Christ. Certainly that's not meant literally. It's a metaphor. It seeks to open our eyes to something that we wouldn't see without a metaphor. Metaphors change our perception. Everyone knows that someone who keeps saying that human beings are dressed-up monkeys will soon experience his fellow men and women as monkeys. And anyone who keeps saying that the world is a madhouse will soon discover sheer madness – even if he lives in a university. But what can we discover with the metaphor of the body of Christ? What changes if we see others and ourselves in the light of this metaphor?

There was already a dispute about this among the Corinthians. The letters of Paul often provoked great debates. Let's listen to one such debate in our imagination, a debate in three stages, with speech and counter-speech.

The first to speak is Titius Justus, a descendant of the Roman colonists who a century previously had refounded Corinth, then totally destroyed. The metaphor of the body is familiar to him. It means a city or a state, a *polis*, a *civitas*.

He says: 'The metaphor of the body of Christ reminds me of the fable of Menenius Agrippa, who once was once a great politician in Rome. After the end of the monarchy the republic was threatened within by class struggles, and from outside by enemies. By promising a remission of debts the Senate had persuaded the plebeians to serve in the war. But after the war the promise was not kept, so in protest the plebeians went to the holy mountain outside Rome and refused to come back. The senate sent Menenius Agrippa to negotiate with the strikers. And he told them the fable of the stomach and the members:

At a time when the individual human limbs were reflecting and discussing, the other members of the body were annoyed that through their toil and service they did everything for the stomach, and the stomach did nothing but enjoy itself. So they resolved that the hands would no longer convey food to the mouth, the mouth should no longer accept it, the teeth should no longer chew it. In their anger they wanted to tame the stomach through hunger. But at the same time the members and the whole body completely lost their strength. Then it became clear to them that the stomach was also performing its service and was not only nourished but gave nourishment, by making the blood, through which we live and are strong, flow to all parts of the body equally, once it has received its strength through the digestion.

With this parable he succeeded in winning over the plebeians and they returned to the city. Rome was saved.'

With the Corinthian community in mind, Titius Justus continues: 'Among us too there is a dispute. Some of us no longer want to have anything to do with others. Paul wants to bring us together again with his metaphor of the body of Christ. But at one point his fable is the opposite of the political fable. There, as throughout politics, the important thing is for the weaker members to be subordinate to the stronger. The parable is about rule, if need be rule with force. But in his metaphor Paul is saying that where the spirit of Christ fills a community, all the members – and particularly the strongest – submit themselves voluntarily and without compulsion to the weakest member and respect it. Therefore in our community all who are excluded in the city of Corinth – the aliens, the slaves, the women – are members with full rights. What is impossible (or not yet possible) in political reality is practised among us. As the body of Christ our community is to be an alternative model for city and state.'

Justus has come to an end. Then his wife Justa speaks. She was born in Athens. Although she is clearly contradicting her husband in what she says, she introduces her view in a very friendly way. 'I just want to add a little detail. The fable of Menenius Agrippa had a consequence: the establishment of the tribunate of the people. From now on the weaker members of the state could defend themselves against attacks from above through the veto of the tribune of the people. So in politics, too, the metaphor of the body and its members can be used in favour of the weak. For example, in Athens Solon ensured that any citizen could make a complaint on behalf of others if he saw someone else being struck, disparaged or maltreated. And his explanation was this. Citizens must become used to 'feeling themselves so to speak as members of a body and empathizing with one another'. And Plato pleaded for holding possessions in common, so that if one member suffered, all suffered. So you see there are some ideas in politics which come closer to our metaphor of the body of Christ than others. There are political programmes which come closer to our community than others. And we must support these. The Holy Spirit, which makes the community the body of Christ, has parallels in the human spirit wherever it supports humanity and solidarity. So as a Christian community we shouldn't just be the opposite of the civil community. We should attempt to support whatever in the civil community within existing possibilities most corresponds to the spirit of Christ.'

Stephanus, an immigrant from Asia Minor, present-day Turkey, introduces the next round of speeches. He says: 'In the human community we mustn't think only of individual states and cities. The whole world is our home, the whole world is our *polis*. We are cosmopolitans. Everything that exists is a member of a great organic whole. So let's live in harmony with nature. We Christians differ from others only because our eyes have been opened to these wider connections through Christ. Through him we again discover that everything is God's creation and that everything belongs together: atoms and molecules, plants and animals, human beings and nature. If we live together organically in the body of Christ, we realize the hidden law of all creation. For the whole world is a body.'

However, his wife Stephanie contradicts him. She says: 'I don't see your marvellous harmony in the world. When we emigrated we were strangers everywhere, people whom others were glad to see the back of. Where are these citizens of the world, who accept everyone as brother and sister? Where are they, when aliens and refugees are being pushed around everywhere? And is it different in nature? Don't we find all over nature a shabby fight over territory; competition for better chances of procreation; shoving and biting over the pecking order; eat or be eaten? Are we to take that as a model? Never! Nature isn't a great organic body that you can snuggle up to. But perhaps it can become that. Perhaps it is the task of the Christian community to be the advance guard of a new creation.'

Finally Aquila, an emigrant from Rome, opens the third round of speeches. He takes up what the politicians and ecologists have said before him: 'If you want the order of the community to be realized symbolically in city and country and even to be an advance post of a renewed creation, then hand, foot and eye must be directed towards the great goal. Didn't Jesus say, "If your eye offends you, pluck it out"? We needn't take that seriously, but it's clear that self-discipline is necessary if anyone wants to be a soldier of Christ. And what do we see? Our community consists of paralysed and limping soldiers of Christ. There are people who sleep with anyone they fancy. There are Christians who go to law against one another. There are brothers who intrigue against others by going to Paul with letters and rumours. Then there are some who regard their incomprehensible talk as profundity from the Holy Spirit. And some become arrogant because they have been taken on a religious trip to the seventh heaven. How can such a community be a powerful army for Christ? How can it be a model for the world? Or even the advance guard for a new world? Isn't it itself a sick member of society? So first of all each individual must be converted. If need be, we must separate from some sick members – and then perhaps we will again become the body of Christ, his hands, his feet, his organs.'

Now it's Prisca's turn to correct her husband. She is often better than him in debate. People whisper to one another. Aquila tried to persuade Paul's scribe at some point to insert an admonition into his letters: if women contradict their husbands, they should do so at home, and not in public. There married women should keep quiet. Things were as human as that in Corinth. So this Prisca says: 'Paul certainly didn't mean that we should separate from our weak members. He says the opposite: all members have a gift. All have a charisma. All contribute to our community life. The metaphor of the body of Christ is an invitation also to discover a positive force in the weakest members. It's not a programme to change them, far less a programme to separate from them if they won't change. It isn't even a programme to help them, for with help one can also humiliate others. No, the metaphor of the body of Christ is meant to open our eyes to the fact that even the weakest members are full of power if the spirit of Christ fills them.'

If Prisca could speak to us today, she would probably choose the following examples. There are now many people who come from Eastern Europe in our churches. Unfriendly comments about their arrival are often made in public, even by people who put social concern high in their party programme. But these very migrants are a blessing: they bring an evangelical piety with them, but without the aggressiveness of fundamentalists. We have this experience with Christians from all over the world, from Korea, Africa or South America. They are more evangelical in their theology. But they come to us and they also want to learn something from quite liberal fellow-Christians. They are ready to have a conversation with them. I want to tell them all, 'You're welcome here as members in the body of Christ. You bring with you something that can be a blessing. It's good that you're here.'

My second example is this. We have long kept quiet about the fact that Christians – including many pastors, men and women – fail in their marriages and their relationships. Yet their experience is a treasure house of suffering and wisdom that we shouldn't hide. How many pastors could help members of their churches because they themselves have suffered the crises in relationships that others go through? So I say, 'All of you who are experiencing crises, separations and divorces, you're welcome. You bring something that others don't have. It can become a blessing for us all.'

My third example is quite different yet again. At present Christian communities are arguing how they should deal with their gay and lesbian members. Some say, 'It's a sin.' Others say, 'It's a sin to say it's a sin.' In short, the debate is very perplexing. But at the beginning of any dialogue should come the acknowledgment of one fact. There are and always have been homosexual members among us. They make a positive contribution to our community life. Some invest in social concerns energies which others put into a family and children – also to our advantage. They deserve our gratitude. To them, too, I would like to say, 'You're welcome among us. You've a charisma. Those of you who survive in the Christian community, indeed invest positively in it, at least have a charisma. To live in our midst despite so many shrill tones you must be very generous, very mature, very understanding towards those who find you so difficult. So please stay with us.'

My fourth example is on a quite different level. Medicine has made much progress. It allows many people to survive when formerly that would have been impossible. But as a result, it leaves an increasing number of people in great uncertainty: how long will it be before the illness recurs, whether it's a cancer or a psychotic phase? It leaves more and more people with the certainty that the rest of their lives will be possible only with limitations. Many of these people live among us. They're valuable. Think of the great strength that they have to develop to regain self-confidence and confidence in life. To all of them I say, 'You're valuable members of the body of Christ. Often you're the strong ones, and we healthy people are the weak ones. We're glad that you're among us. Stay with us.'

I could give many more examples. Time and again it's the case that where Christ's spirit takes hold of people who are on the margins, who have limitations, who are regarded as weak, weakness is turned into strength, suffering into blessing. If we are bound together in the spirit of Christ and deal with our members, strong and weak, in this spirit, then we will become convincing.

Then perhaps we will also convince the city and the state in which we live that it is better to support the weak members than to weaken them further. Today it isn't the plebeians who emigrate, but the rich with their money. And they don't go to sacred mountains, but to tax havens. They say to us: If you make your society as anti-social as possible and as profit-orientated as necessary, then we will return – provided that you've demolished the welfare state. Dear people, don't get infected with this spirit. This spirit of social chill will lead to disaster. First the weak will be isolated; then they will feel no obligations to society and criminality will rise. Meanwhile the rich will have become sufficiently rich and influential to set up a police state. Beyond any doubt we must get a better balance between rights and what the high-flyers can force through. But this will come about only if we integrate the weak members of our society and don't exclude them.

And we don't need only to convince society. We must convince ourselves as a church and a community. Nowadays the church is regarded as a sick member of society. In modern times, all other areas have experienced a tremendous increase in efficiency: science, business, law and politics – though politics perhaps only to a limited degree. However, for too long now the churches haven't experienced any spirit of renewal. And even if they did, they could hardly keep up with the increasing efficiency in modern times. But there perhaps is our opportunity. Where everything has to be perfect, where social fitness becomes the decisive factor in any biography, it's good for there to be at least one group which remembers that it is a law of humanity to be imperfect and not perfect. The spirit of Christ makes us certain that God accepts imperfect people regardless of their achievements and without prior conditions.

But finally, each of us must convince himself or herself. And that's often the hardest thing. In all of us there is something that is homeless and uprooted. Give it a home in you. Accept the alien into you – not least so that you can turn to the aliens around you.

In each of us there is someone who has failed in relationships. And that's painful. No one here is perfect. So let the pain into you. Then you won't carry it into every new relationship.

In all of us there are sexual impulses and fantasies which don't correspond to what our world and above all what we ourselves regard as a norm. Don't be afraid of them. In this particular sphere there's a big terrorist word, and that's 'normal'.

In all of us there is a fear of illness, handicap and death. Accept this fear too. Acknowledge your weak side, if only so as to be more aware of every day on which you are without handicap and pain, or on which you experience less handicap and pain than usual.

In each of us there is a sad corner in which a depressive crouches – somewhere in the areas of our life – for one person in the cellar, for another in the living room; in some as a permanent lodger, in others as an eerie guest. That too is part of life. How can we understand other people and help them if we have no inkling of how helpless one is when one stands alongside one's own life and it seems to be buried?

The spirit of Christ, the Holy Spirit, whose festival we celebrate at Pentecost, is the great power which can turn weakness into strength, suffering into blessing, and restore us to life from the tomb of depression. This spirit makes us capable of recognizing something of ourselves in others, however bizarre, and discovering in ourselves something of others, however strange it may seem to us. It brings us together. It makes us rejoice over every gift, every competence, every charisma. It makes us suffer with all that suffers pain. It gives us the certainty that where this spirit fills our hearts, the dawn radiance of a new world is already shining here and now.

And may the peace of God, which surpasses all our understanding, keep your hearts in Christ Jesus. Amen.

The Weaker Members as the Strength of the Body of Christ

This sermon was given in St Peter's Church, Heidelberg at Pentecost, on 26 May 1996, as part of a series on the eight hundredth anniversary of the city of Heidelberg. It was entitled 'Seek the Best for the City. The Task of Christians between Heaven and Earth'. The fable of Menenius Agrippa appears in Livy, *Ab urbe condita* II, 32,8ff.; it is given here in an abbreviated form. Plutarch, *Solon* 18, reports on Solon's reform, using the metaphor of the body and its members. On 25 January and 23 February 1996 the *Guidelines of the Council of the Evangelical Church in Germany on Homosexuality and the Church* were approved, under the title 'Living with Tensions'. This maintains a rejection of homosexuality in principle, but accepts its ethical formation positively as a task. This is an oppressively contradictory document which makes a little progress, because in some circumstances homosexual pastors are accepted. But all in all, it is more evidence of a moral paralysis because of incompatible positions, with a fatal message to those concerned: they will be accepted only on condition that they do not accept part of themselves. The sermon alludes to the state elections in Baden-Württemberg in 1996, in which the Social Democrats attacked migrants from East European countries and lost not only the election, but also some of their integrity.

'My Strength is Made Perfect in Weakness'

A sermon for a child and for church elders

(II Corinthians 12.1–10)

I must boast; there is nothing to be gained by it, but I will go on to visions and revelations of the Lord. I know a man in Christ who fourteen years ago was caught up to the third heaven – whether in the body or out of the body I do not know, God knows. And I know that this man was caught up into Paradise – whether in the body or out of the body I do not know, God knows – and he heard things that cannot be told, which man may not utter. On behalf of this man I will boast, but on my own behalf I will not boast, except of my weaknesses. Though if I wished to boast, I would not be a fool, for I would be speaking the truth. But I refrain from it, so that no one may think more of me than he sees in me or hears from me. And to keep me from being too elated by the abundance of revelations, a thorn was given me in the flesh, a messenger of Satan, to harass me, to keep me from being too elated. Three times I besought the Lord about this, that it should leave me; but he said to me, 'My grace is sufficient for you, for my strength is made perfect in weakness.' Therefore I will all the more gladly boast of my weaknesses, in insults, hardships, persecutions, and calamities for Christ's sake; for when I am weak, then I am strong.

Today we have two tasks: we are baptizing a child, and we are instituting new church elders. We are baptizing this child in the name of the Father and the Son and the Holy Spirit.

What does it mean when we baptize it in the name of the Father? We are born into this world without anyone asking us whether we want to be or not. We are born into a family which we haven't sought, a country which we haven't decided on, a body which we haven't chosen. We can accept all that as blind fate. But we can also receive this life as a gift of God and as a task: that we are called to the freedom of the children of God. Therefore we baptize in the name of the Father.

We baptize this child in the name of the Son. What does that mean? This child is secure in the love of its parents. They give it courage to live. But later, time and again this courage will be crucified and buried in crises. So we give this child a friend and brother along life's way, Jesus, so that someone is near even in the darkest hours of life. With Jesus we are crucified and buried in order to begin a new life already now in the power of his resurrection.

We baptize this child in the name of the Holy Spirit. What does that mean? This child comes into a world full of unholy spirit, a spirit of hatred and prejudice, cynicism and social chill. But we want its life to be permeated by the Holy Spirit: by the spirit of reconciliation and peace, the spirit of confidence, the spirit of the Christian community, the spirit of Jesus. Therefore we baptize it in the name of the Holy Spirit.

After the baptism

We have baptized a child. We all wish the little one well on its further way through life. Perhaps some people implicitly expect that baptism will help to realize this wish, that it will be a protection against illness and danger, and ward off the evil in the world. But in our minds we know better: baptism and faith are no protection against illness and disease. Rather, being a Christian and faith are a way of dealing with illness and crises. Our text shows that. It speaks of a sick apostle, of Paul in crisis.

His community expected that he, the apostle, would be filled with mysterious power which would protect them from all evil; that he would spread happiness in life and heal the sick. And what did they find? That the apostle himself was sick, a broken man. What disease did he have? Paul speaks of blows from an angel of Satan, a thorn in the flesh. The Greek church fathers, who still heard many undertones in his language which we find it difficult, if not impossible, to reconstruct, agreed in their diagnosis: the apostle had migraines, pains like blows to his head. It was as if someone was hammering a nail through his brain. Paul couldn't always cope. And was this an apostle? Good God! An apostle was meant to win people over – and how could he do that when he was sometimes a picture of human misery? An apostle was meant to heal sick people. How could he do that when he himself was sick? An apostle was meant to act positively, think positively, speak positively. Paul wasn't positive enough.

What does the apostle say to that?. He writes that he too has positive things to offer. Top religious experiences. First-class nearness to God. Ecstasy taking him to the third heaven. But he doesn't want to offer that. He stands apart from these top experiences, so apart that they seem to have happened to other people.

I can well understand why he speaks in such a detached way of himself. At the high points of life we are often outside ourselves, no longer in ourselves. There is music which is so beautiful that one floats in it and thinks that one has come home. There are spring days when life rises anew, even when it already seems exhausted. There is an erotic fascination which transports us into another state: second-class nearness to heaven. But when do we feel most that we are irreplaceably ourselves, tied to this one body, thrown into this unique life? We feel it when things go badly with us, when our own pain or the suffering of others hits us, when an illness lays us low. Then we no longer want to be ourselves; we want to be different, to have another body, another life. And then we have to learn: That is your life. That is your body. That is what you are.

I know that there are people among us who have good reason to wish that they could live their lives again from the beginning, like the life of this child whom we have baptized. If only I could have another body, one which no longer gave me pain, one in which I didn't suffer!

Paul was like this. He wanted to be someone else. His illness was like a thorn in his life, an open wound. And his critics in the community irritated this wound. They wanted another apostle. And so in fact did he. He secretly felt that they were right. Three times he prayed to God, 'Make me healthy. It isn't fair to give me a great task – and not the body to carry it out with.' But he received only one certainty, only one answer: 'Let my grace be sufficient for you, for my strength is powerful in weakness.' Or, translated literally: my strength is made perfect in weakness or illness. (The Greek word for weakness is the same as that for illness.)

And he wrote all this to the Corinthian community to defend himself against the charge that he was so far from being positive, was powerful only in letters, painful in his speeches, repulsive in appearance. How did the community react to this letter? Let's listen to three voices from it. First Skolops, a critic of Paul. Then Luke the physician, his friend. And finally Apollos, at the same time his colleague, friend and critic.

We shouldn't imagine Skolops as a sinister character. He was very committed to the community. But this letter made him indignant. 'Yet more moral extortion,' he grumbles. 'This Paul always wants to be first. He wanted to surpass everyone even when he was still a Jew. And now he's doing the same thing in Christianity. He's reprimanded Peter, he's reprimanded Apollos, and now he's reprimanded the missionaries whom we received. He simply can't grasp that in some respects they're more attractive than he is. He must always be on top, always the first. So he can't bear to be sick and weak.

We care for the sick and the weak in our community. We also care for the sick Paul. What I mean is simply that such sick and weak people needn't necessarily be at the head of the community. There we need people who can talk well, people who can take on burdens and are healthy, people whom we can also point out to outsiders.

No, really we don't have anything against Paul. But if he exploits his illness to build up his influence, if he wants to suggest to all of us, "Look, with my suffering I am nearer to Christ than you are", if he misuses compassion to disarm his critics, then I protest.'

But Luke the physician defends his friend. 'Does his sickness disturb you? It's disturbed and tormented Paul far more. He has laboriously learned to accept it. That was a long learning process, in three stages.

At first he saw this illness only as an enemy: an angel of Satan was behind it, an evil being to torment him. One can only fight such an enemy; one can't accept it.

Then he learned to understand his sickness as a kind of education. Perhaps it was perhaps meant to keep him from being arrogant, to make him ready for once to be the last and the next to last, which of course he always found difficult. But this thorn in the flesh was given to him for precisely that purpose.

But Paul reached the third stage when he fully accepted his sickness. Then it was clear to him that he had to live with it. Then he understood the sickness as an opportunity to bear witness with his body to a power which didn't come from him: to the strength of God which is made perfect in weakness.

So please respect Paul. He is a human being as we are. How is he to accept his thorn in the flesh if we don't accept it?'

Apollos is the last to speak. He is a philosophical brain who always reduces everything to basic principles. And he wants to do this once again, not least to get the discussion away from Paul a bit.

'Dear people,' he says, 'a truth which is important for every individual shines out in the apostle's illness. God's power is strong in the weak; no conditions are attached to God's grace. It's there not only for people who are strong but also for people who are weak; not only for those who succeed in everything but also for others whose life has gone wrong in many ways. It's there not only for those who come, see and conquer, but for the many who languish, stand in the shadows and waste away: not only for the great, but for the small.

God's power is strong in the weak – that's also important for the community. A Christian community is not a community of the perfect, but a drama with mixed characters – with people in whom light and shade are closely connected. We need people to lead the community who know from their own experience that there are deep shadows in life. For that's one of the basic truths of Christianity: one doesn't have to ascend to heaven to be near to God. We find God down here – in real life, in all people. God's power is active in weak people. Therefore we shouldn't encourage any rivalry in the community over who has got furthest up the heavenly ladder, to be near to God. Nor should there be any rivalry over who has descended deepest to hell. God is everywhere, in the heights and in the depths, where we celebrate the ecstatic high points of life and where we descend to the depths of pain.

God's power is strong in the weak – that's important for the whole world, precisely because we live in a world in which the weak have difficulties. The big animals eat the little ones. The strong displace the others from the food trough. Here the rule applies, 'If you aren't fit, you don't get it.' But we human beings have taken a step into a new world which already begins in the midst of this old world. There this rule no longer applies. There the weak are helped. There everyone is the same, great or small.

We often doubt whether we've really taken this step. We doubt it when we hear how foreigners and asylum-seekers are treated in our country, how the handicapped are increasingly frequently being maltreated. Or when we see pictures from Yugoslavia, Afghanistan or southern Sudan. There again we find the old bestial rule: 'If you aren't fit, you don't get it.'

If you doubt whether we can get beyond the 'eat or be eaten' of animals, baptism reminds you. It's a sign that we're called to a life in another spirit. It's a sign that an image of God is hidden in every human being, that all are equal before God. No Christian is more baptized than another.

No pope, no bishop, no theologian, no pastor, no chapter member is more baptized than the child whom we have just baptized.

No Federal Chancellor, no minister, no leader is more an image of God than each one of us. You are all God's children, called to God's freedom, which no one can take from you. God's image remains in all of you, even in illnesses and crises.

You all have this task: 'Seek my face.' And you will find God's face in a small child, a beloved person, in the strong and the weak, near and far, happy and unhappy, all over the world, in Germany and in China.

And may the peace of God, which surpasses all our understanding, keep your hearts in Christ Jesus. Amen.

This sermon was given in St Peter's Church, Heidelberg on 6 February 1994. The text was fixed as a result of planning and advertising, as three other tasks were bound up with the service, first of all a baptism. The text that the parents wanted was: 'You have said, "Seek my face. Therefore your face, Lord, I seek"' (Ps.27.8). The family was living in China at the time and was only in Germany, their homeland, for a short period. At the same time the newly-elected church elders (or 'chapter members') were being instituted to office. Finally, the student orchestra had chosen this Sunday to structure the service around a Haydn symphony. The sermon could not do justice to all the tasks and concerns at the same time.

Love as a Sign of Life

On the imperfection of the perfect bond

(Colossians 3.12–15)

Put on, then, as God's chosen ones, holy and beloved, compassion, kindness, lowliness, meekness and patience, forbearing one another and, if one has a complaint against another, forgiving one another; as the Lord has forgiven you, so you also must forgive. And above all these put on love, which binds everything together in perfect harmony. And let the peace of Christ rule in your hearts, to which indeed you were called in the one body. And be thankful.

In a book of children's 'letters to God' I found the following question: 'Dear God, our neighbours keep quarrelling so loudly. Can't you make sure that only people who are nice to each other marry? People who really love each other? Yours, Sabine.'

What are we grown-ups, as parents, to reply to that? A first attempt at an answer would be: You've discovered a contradictory truth: disputes bind people together. They bind some people together so perfectly that they couldn't get on without a dispute. It's a complicated way of loving each other. But it's very exhausting, and I wouldn't wish it for you. However, there is such a thing as a typical quarrelsome marriage.

A second attempt at an answer is: Are you certain that they only love each other *a little*? Perhaps they love, or have loved, each other too much. They've expected everything of the other: the fulfilment of their life and their most secret longings. But these very great expectations have not been fulfilled. Every time they see each other, this great disappointment reawakens in them, because the great longing for the other is still alive in them. Perhaps it would be better for them if they loved each other less – hoped, desired, expected less of each other; if they were more content with their own limitations and those of the other. They are perhaps a typical disappointed romantic marriage.

A third answer could be: they still love each other. There is no lack of mutual fondness. But they can't cope with their everyday life. Feeling love in everyday life involves more than liking each other. One must be able to deal with time, with money and with promises.
– Dealing with time, particularly when it's short, in the morning between coffee and the timetable.
– Dealing with each other: paying the boring bills for taxes and utilities before spending money on a much more interesting hobby.
– Dealing with little promises: being back for supper in the evening and not keeping the whole family waiting. – When children are there, above all being able to cope with them, and not seeing them as a terrible attack on one's own freedom and leisure-time.

Often enough there is no lack of love and affection. There is often simply a lack of everyday organization. That's the problem of a typical chaotic marriage.

And finally a fourth answer: perhaps the neighbours really no longer know whether they love each other. They discover how different they are. At the beginning little irritations were an incentive to cover them with even greater love. But it's like having a very small stone in your shoe. If you walk a mile you hardly notice it. But if you walk twenty miles it ruins your foot. And life is a long walk: more than twenty miles. What was no problem to begin with can finally ruin life together. Many people notice only too late where they are rubbing each other up the wrong way. What was previously a bond of love is then suddenly experienced as chains – the moment when they start being a strain. Some manage to become reconciled, at a distance. That can lead to a sympathetic and stable marriage of respect. But it can also lead to separation.

I don't suppose that all these answers would satisfy Sabine. Isn't there already a good deal of the resignation of adulthood in discovering signs of love even in the strangest relationships? Our children long for more. Sabine would have sufficient reason to write a new letter.

Dear God,
My parents say that even people who aren't nice to each other love each other. I don't understand that. That can't be so. I've two arguments. First, my parents are really nice to each other. Secondly, in your book you write, 'Love one another, for love is the bond of perfection.' That was the marriage text for Granny and Grandpa. And they were also nice to each other. Are you a romantic? Perhaps you're asking too much of people. My father sometimes says that you shouldn't have written in your book, 'What God has joined together let no man put asunder', but, 'What God has not joined together man should not hold together.' I believe that my father thinks you're a romantic.
With love,
Sabine

How are we to reply to that? Is God a romantic? Doesn't God love people unconditionally? One might ask how he can bear it when one thinks of all the atrocities that human beings commit. But he is God, and we are human beings. Our love can always be only a human and imperfect echo of his unconditional love. It can't be as perfect as God's love. So a fine saying like 'And above all these put on love, which binds everything together in perfect harmony' is to some degree open to misunderstanding. Three misunderstandings need to be corrected.

The first is that in the world of the letter the word 'perfect' means something like what we would call a fulfilled life. We don't just want to live; we want to be fulfilled. Many people seek fulfilment in little ecstasies beyond everyday life. Many seek more-than-just-living in eroticism, others in esoteric experiences – in penetrating spheres of life which point beyond our normal world. Something like that was also the fashion then. Some people sought secret esoteric experiences – by entering heaven to join with the angels in worshipping God already. The author of the letter says to such people: fulfilled life lies not only in transportations to heaven (or erotic ecstasies in heaven), but in love on earth, in everyday life.

The second correction is that the author of the letter doesn't mean specifically erotic love, but love in all relationships. He's not just speaking to people in love. That love fulfils life is true both for single and married people, the divorced and the widowed, those who live together and those who live alone. It's true for all forms of life, but it's also true of marriage. Here we need the same fairness, the same talk, the same consideration in dealing with one another as anywhere else. There's a modern myth that only erotic relationships are really fulfilling.

For me the third correction is the most important one. What the text calls 'perfection' and 'fulfilment' is intended for imperfect people – including people who are far away from themselves and a fulfilled life. Immediately before our fine saying we read: 'forbearing one another and, if one has a complaint against another, forgiving each other; as the Lord has forgiven you, so you also must forgive.' This perfection manifests itself in the way in which we deal with our imperfection, with the imperfection of the other. And not only that.

First of all a marriage is an invitation to learn how to deal with one's own imperfections. For before we bind ourselves to someone else in a marriage we live all our lives in a marriage to ourselves – in other words to a notoriously imperfect person. For many people this marriage to ourselves is a quarrelsome marriage. We grumble at ourselves. We don't treat ourselves well. We don't forgive ourselves our mistakes or even concede them, because we don't want to forgive ourselves. Those who have lived in a quarrelsome marriage to themselves find it difficult to live in a marriage to someone else, and their partners often find it even more difficult. But they also have a chance of getting out of this quarrel with themselves, when the other assures them, 'I love you, I want you.' Then this grumbling can stop of its own accord.

Many people live in a romantic marriage to themselves. They have great dreams of what their life should look like – and these dreams are all a size too big. Some people never get over the hurt that comes with bringing life back to reality. Those who live in a romantic marriage to themselves find it difficult when living with someone else to discover the wisdom that you can't be happy despite yourself but only with yourself; you can't fight your nature, you have to live with it. But a marriage can also be an opportunity to get over this romantic relationship to our-selves, if we believe that our partner loves us as we are, and not just as we dream of being.

Many people live in a chaotic marriage to themselves. They don't order their time, but get caught up in ever new entangle-ments which exceed their chronological budget. They're driven by ever new desires which ask too much of their financial budget. And they keep changing their minds, so that nothing that they say can be relied on. A marriage is a great invitation (and also an opportunity) to put that in order too. But for many people it is also a school for learning to be more tolerant of some chaos.

Finally, many people live in a marriage to themselves of detached respect. They don't let much get to them, so as not to make themselves vulnerable. But they too are sometimes weak, confused, helpless. They too aren't always just people to look up to. In each of them there is a small boy or a small girl who sometimes simply wants to be comforted: hugged, not kept at a distance. We look for and need a place where we may show that we too are weak and vulnerable – without being exploited. And marriage can be such a place.

Now in all this, love between human beings is simply an echo of the love of God: God knows our quarrel with ourselves, our romantic dreams, our inner chaos, our weakness behind the façade of strength. God accepts us without preconditions – far beyond what any spouse could bear.

So what are we to say to our children when they ask us, 'Why are you grown-ups often unkind to each other? Why do you wage such terrible little wars against each other in everyday life?' I want to end by attempting an answer – an answer for children and grown-ups, for in each of us there is a child longing for love. All are children of God!

Dear children, dear people, it's always sad when people quarrel and separate. You experience it often today and will probably experience it even more frequently in the future. But for once, look at it the other way round. It really is a miracle how many people stay together. Really it's quite improbable that two people should make an alliance for life. Really it's a riddle that with all the human tendency to degenerate there is so much love between them. One can't say that those who get on well together are better people. When I get on well with my wife, when no doors bang between us and no words fly round the house like missiles, it's a great happiness for which I am thankful – as thankful as I am for life generally. And I don't deserve it.

Unfortunately we human beings can't get love to order. Love is spontaneous, a sovereign expression of life in which we detect God at work. But precisely for that reason we may not content ourselves with saying, 'It's either there or not. Some people are lucky, others not.' No, because it's spontaneously there, we must at least keep rediscovering it. We must perceive it and be grateful for it. So even in the most troubled relationships I still look for trace elements of love – even in a quarrelsome marriage, a disappointed romantic marriage, a chaotic marriage. One simply has to have an eye for them. The greater the lovelessness, the more striking those trace elements of love are. The greater the darkness, the easier it is to recognize a small spark of love in it and to transform everything even with a little candle that one lights.

Our responsibility is to preserve love as a precious gift. Gratitude for love keeps it alive – gratitude which one communicates, which one lets the other detect.

Today is an opportunity for all of us to practise a little of this gratitude. When two people are joined together in a marriage, although there is no compulsion about it today, they express the fact that there is love which is sufficiently certain of itself to dare to reach for a whole life. Today two people are making an alliance for life.

But we should all feel encouraged silently to renew our alliance with life: the promise to perceive love even where the world is dark and cold, the promise to hand on love even where there is no love, and above all the intention to be grateful for love and all that love brings to fulfilment; for love in its many forms between human beings.

It is no coincidence that the passage from which our marriage text comes continues with the invitation 'Be thankful.' Let me read it once again:

> And above all these put on love, which binds everything together in perfect harmony. And let the peace of Christ rule in your hearts, to which indeed you were called in the one body. And be thankful.

And may this peace of God which surpasses all our understanding keep your hearts and minds in Christ Jesus. Amen.

This sermon was given at a marriage service in the Providence Church, Heidelberg on 26 August 1995. The child's letter to God is taken, with slight alterations, from B.V. Issendorff, *Gott kann nicht Urlaub machen. Antworten auf die Kinderbriefe an den lieben Gott*, Gütersloh 1979. The view that love is a 'sovereign expression of life' and that precisely such sovereign or 'spontaneous' expressions of life are pointers to God's goodness in creation is inspired by the Danish philosopher of religion and theologian K.E. Lagstrup, *Norm und Spontaneität. Ethik und Politik zwischen Technik und Dilettantokratie*, Tübingen 1989.

Level-headedness as a Sign of Love

On the courage to marry

(II Timothy 1.7)

For God did not give us a spirit of timidity but a spirit of power and love and self-control.

You need courage to marry. Certainly there are many wise books on marriage which seek to give us courage to marry, but often, contrary to their purpose, they disseminate a spirit of fear.

The first fear is that with marriage habit will creep in and make love die the slow death of the everyday.

The second fear is that with marriage what was freely given affection will become an obligation. That provokes resistance in us. We don't want a life run by rules.

The third fear is that with marriage we will be led astray into being unfaithful to ourselves. Who can make a promise now for the person we shall become in ten, twenty or thirty years? Mustn't we always violate this future person a little if we bind ourselves for the whole of our lives?

The fourth fear is that with marriage, life will be restricted. It won't just run on predictable lines. It must also become more predictable to give children and family a sphere of life that they can rely on.

And finally, in all these fears, the one great fear. Marriage will set in motion the statistic which says that many marriages fail. And everyone knows that this leaves behind wounds and scratches. Often these hurt all life long.

We have developed something of a phobia about marriage. It would be good if there were a therapy for that, as there is for phobias about dogs. Anyone who is afraid of dogs has to take a dog out every day and stroke it at least once: he or she will soon discover that one can live with dogs. It's different with fear of marriage. We aren't afraid of this or that; in the end we're afraid of ourselves. The advice to go for a walk together every day and stroke each other more than just once isn't wrong, but it doesn't solve our problem.

Formerly, marriage used to be not just about love but very much more about safeguarding existence, work, inheritance and social respectability. Nowadays all that is fading into the background. Today marriage is about ourselves, our lives – this unique, precious and wonderful life. And if we're afraid in all this, we're afraid about this one life.

Therefore here we don't have to do only with our partner; we're also confronted with the one who gives and takes this unique life, with God. We're confronted with a voice which says to us, 'What are you doing with your life? And how do you relate to another life which is just as unique and valuable as your own? Will you say yes to this one person in precisely the same way as you affirm your own life? Will you bind yourself as firmly to this other person as you are bound to yourself – all your life?'

If we bind ourselves to another person in this way before God, then we're going beyond all that legislators and lawyers say about marriage. We're going beyond all the rules formulated by churches and moralists, beyond all the expectation that the world around has of us. All that is important, and no one can completely avoid it. But before God a marriage is made in a sphere in which no this-worldly authority can make a pronouncement: no registrar, no lawyer, no pastor. Then even friends fall back and parents have no more to say here. Only the two partners say their yes to each other – in a hidden corner of their life, into which only God can look. And without this hidden inner yes, which only God hears, the outward yes that we can also hear isn't worth much. If two people say yes to one another in this most hidden inner depth, then the spirit of God dwells in them.

And precisely that is my wish for you, that your marriage may be guided in the spirit of God and be grounded where no human beings can interfere. You've chosen for yourself a marriage text which speaks of this spirit of God: 'God did not give us a spirit of timidity but a spirit of power and love and level-headedness.'

At the beginning of this sentence there is a negative statement: God's spirit is not a spirit of fear. Rather, you are assured that nothing in the world ultimately has power over you – except the one who has made the whole world. With this marriage text you are saying that your marriage is made in a sphere which escapes any social control – in that sphere where we are alone with God, where all other voices fall silent, where we are free. God's spirit frees us from the fear of what others say and think.

The text makes three positive statements about this spirit of freedom: it is a spirit of power and love and level-headedness.

It is a spirit of power. One needs power in marriage – above all power to work on oneself and to change oneself. Of course one can practise a marriage like two parallel lines: they never change their direction. But they never touch either, until infinity. However, in a marriage one needs to touch more often – time and again, not just once, not just where two straight lines intersect, and certainly not just in infinity. What follows from that? One must keep changing the direction of one's straight line to get back together. One must sometimes even take what from outside look like oblique ways to get back together again. And that becomes even more exciting when there aren't just two lines, but three or four; when a baby writes a line in your shared book of life – or scribbles across it with a broad felt-tip – and later when the marks of a second child are added. Think how many changes of course are necessary in order not to get separated. But at the same time, think how many gentle curves make life a delight because by following them one keeps getting closer. All that requires strength and courage – above all strength and courage for oneself.

But here you have an ally, God. God follows all our ways,

whether straight or meandering. God remains faithful to us through many curves and bends, regardless of whether we live alone or as a couple, with or without children, happy or sad. Certainly we human beings can't be as faithful to one another as God is faithful to us – God, who keeps giving even the greatest villain a chance to repent and to change his life. But our love may be the imperfect copy of his love. Our yes to life, to our partner, to our children and friends, may be a copy of God's great Yeses.

And therefore the spirit of God is, secondly, a spirit of love. In wishing you this spirit of love, my wish is that you will always know that you *yourselves* are loved before you begin to love others. Every human being is God's idea. Something unique is present in the world with each one of us. There are certainly people who think that they must be God's nightmare, because their lives seem to be so confused and chaotic. But it is marvellous when even they become certain that they too are a good idea of God's, that it is good that they exist. Anyone who turns to God in this way every day is always having birthdays: every day such people may be glad that they are there and that others are also there. This is the joy I mean when I say that I wish you the spirit of love, that you may know that you are always loved before you begin to love. Then neither need keep putting the other to the test: do you love me, do you really love me?

For so many tests of love unintentionally ask too much. Do you know the story of the little trout and the tadpole? They're in love with one another, since they grew up together in the same pond. But then the tadpole turned into a frog and hopped on to the land. And he said to his friend, the trout, 'Come to land too.' But the trout protested, 'I can't, I'm a fish.' Then the frog pressed her, 'Do you love me or not?' 'Of course I love you,' said the trout. 'Then,' said the frog, 'come to me immediately.' And for sheer love the trout leapt on to the land and her love ended tragically. She died.

What can we learn from that? In some marriages one person

proves to be a frog and the other a trout. If one uses that as a reproach all life long, one makes life very difficult. Someone who loves another only on condition that the fish becomes a frog or the frog becomes a fish is no longer acting in the spirit of love. This spirit gives us the certainty that every human being is an idea of God – sometimes more fish, and sometimes more frog.

Thirdly, the spirit of God is a spirit of level-headedness. And here too we do best to begin with ourselves, namely with the recognition that we are human beings with limitations, with limited capacity, limited competence, limited success, always only with limited charm – and never perfect. We can be content only within our limitations, never contrary to them. That in particular is difficult in marriage. How many marriages are per-meated (and a little poisoned) by the undertow of unfulfilled longings?

Here's a story about that, too. Once upon a time two couples lived opposite on the same street, the Bigs and the Littles. The Bigs were young and dynamic, attractive, sporting people. The Littles were modest and unassuming; they belonged to that adorable species of little grey mice. Mr Little often sat at the window and dreamed: if only I had such a self-confident, out-going wife as Big has. He saw the many smart people who visited them in the evening. He heard of their parties. He regis-tered the signs of popularity and success. But what he didn't know was that on the other side of the street Mr Big often sat there in the evening and dreamed: how marvellous it would be if I had so loving a wife as Little has, a wife who didn't have to be doing something every evening, who just smiled, and you lit up, who didn't need much to be content and who played so nicely with her children. How much more content Big and Little would be if they could decide to live in their minds with the partners they really had, and not with a dream wife. That would be level-headedness: the knowledge that no one is perfect, that no one fulfils every dream, that there are limits everywhere. But unfortunately the story of many couples sounds more like this:

'And if they are not dead, then he still dreams of another wife and she still dreams of another husband.'

Perhaps you've noticed that three times I've emphasized that we must begin with ourselves. We need strength to change *ourselves*, to remain true to others. We need love of *ourselves* in order to be able to give it to others. We need level-headedness about *ourselves* so that we can deal carefully with others. Living together in a marriage calls for a never-ending cultivation of living *with oneself*. In a word, those who get on well with themselves can also get on well with others. They can also live alone.

Some people see it differently. Some people seek *self*-development and *self*-realization without marriage and family – as if they were wasting something of life and neglecting something of themselves if they tied themselves to another. What a mistake! As though one's life without a partner were a life without limits – and as though it were first limited by a marriage.

We are always already tied to something very limited, very vulnerable, very limiting – all our lives: to *ourselves*. We have none of us chosen ourselves. We all find ourselves already married to our lives. The only question is whether we feel this a hindrance or whether we are grateful for our limited lives; whether we say yes to this life, indeed to our covenant with life, indeed to our covenant with God.

Now when this couple say yes to each other, each may repeat this yes as a renewal of his and her covenant with life, which God made with each one of us when he gave us life. Certainly, some of us will find this yes difficult, and others will remember the time when they found it difficult. For yet others, dark times are still to come. But today is a day of celebration. Today two people are confirming their yes to each other – their yes to life and to God, their yes to their child and to their children, and at the same time and first of all their yes to each other. Today everyone may join in saying it – even if fear and anxiety sometimes darken our lives. For the text which this couple have chosen applies not only to them but to all of us: 'God did not give us a spirit of timidity but a spirit of power and love and level-headedness.'

And may this peace of God which surpasses all our understanding keep your hearts and minds in Christ Jesus. Amen.

This sermon was given at a marriage service in St Peter's Church, Heidelberg on 1 April 1995. The story of the trout and the tadpole is a variation on W. Schnurre, 'Die Kaulquappe und der Weissfisch', in H. and U. Halbfass (eds.), *Das Menschenhaus. Ein Lesebuch für den Religionsunterricht*, Düsseldorf 1972, 53.

The Need to Grow in Faith

Why the Letter to the Hebrews rejects a second repentance

(Hebrews 6.9–12)

Though we speak thus, yet in your case, beloved, we feel sure of better things that belong to salvation. For God is not so unjust as to overlook your work and the love which you showed for his sake in serving the saints, as you still do. And we desire each one of you to show the same earnestness in realizing the full assurance of hope until the end, so that you may not be sluggish, but imitators of those who through faith and patience inherit the promises.

The Letter to the Hebrews contains some hard teaching. All the great churches are united in rejecting it. It is the teaching of the impossibility of a second repentance. This says, 'You only have one chance of becoming a Christian. If you go wrong in your faith, allow yourself to be defeated, if you fall away – then you can never begin again.' Then you're like a useless field full of thistles and thorns. That is what the Letter to the Hebrews has said immediately before our text. And our text sounds like a semi-retraction. 'Although we speak so harshly,' it tells readers, 'we are convinced that things are better with you . . . ' That you aren't a field which needs to be burned off, but can bear fruit. That you have a chance.

Although I reject the doctrine that there is only one chance of becoming a Christian, there are two insights in the Letter to the Hebrews with which I agree.

It says that the practice of love provides the certainty of being on the right way. Where Christians help one another, Christianity is not yet lost; here Christians have a chance. Where, as in Hebrews, Christians have lost possessions in persecutions and share what is left, they are on the right way.

Where there is such love, there is also hope and faith. All three key words – love, hope and faith – occur in our text.

And there is a second insight. The Letter to the Hebrews is basically not so much about the danger of apostasy from Christianity as about the danger of stagnating in it. Everyone has heard and understood the first teaching. But if we remain at the first teaching, if we don't progress to a deeper understanding of Christian faith, then we will soon no longer have any faith. It's like riding a bicycle: if one doesn't keep moving forward, one doesn't remain stationary, but tips over. Stagnation is a fall.

Many people today are stagnating in their faith. In their childhood they encountered a faith for which God was the extended arm of parental control, with the promise, 'If you're good, you'll get to heaven.' Or rather more subtly, 'If you behave well, you'll have a successful life.' No wonder that people turn away from this faith, if they don't come across more mature forms of Christian faith or haven't developed such forms themselves. Today the whole church is in danger of being tied by outsiders to such infantile forms of Christian faith.

But what is a mature faith? What does a faith which is inwardly mature and is still growing look like? I could say a good deal about this, but I shall limit myself to three features which emerge from the Letter to the Hebrews.

First, a mature faith is a critical faith which doesn't take over everything from tradition but makes a distinction between what is transitory and what is abiding. The Letter to the Hebrews does precisely that. It makes a distinction in its Bible, the Old Testament, between what is abiding and what God has abolished. It does away with parts of the Bible, e.g. the Old Testament sacrificial laws. We must apply this power of faith to discern and criticize to the New Testament as well. And we have in fact already been doing that for a long time: we do it when, like Luther, we reject the radical teaching of the Letter to the Hebrews that conversion can only happen once, but nevertheless treasure and love the Letter to the Hebrews.

Secondly, a mature faith recognizes the plurality of what is true before God. For God, as the Letter to the Hebrews says, has 'spoken many times and in many ways'. God has spoken by the prophets. God speaks through creation. For it has been created by the word of God. God speaks through the blood of Abel – and through the blood of all innocent victims of murder. God doesn't just speak here. He laments. He cries out. He calls for help. He pronounces the judgment of conscience. According to the Letter to the Hebrews, the word of God is a living sword which pierces every creature. None is hidden from God. Finally, God speaks not only through words but through images. The Letter to the Hebrews reads the Old Testament as a treasure house of profound pictures which point beyond themselves. God speaks and calls in manifold ways. That is confusing for immature people. They find it difficult to put up with contradictions and tensions. The most insecure people have to know, 'It's like that, and not otherwise.'

Thirdly, a mature faith is sure of its identity. It knows that God speaks to us in Jesus in a unique way and that as a result Christian faith becomes something special. Hebrews reflects on this particular feature.

At that time all religions had sacrifices and priests. Christian faith had neither the one nor the other. Hebrews sees this as an advantage. The unique sacrifice of Jesus and the unique self-sacrifice of the high priest make all priests and sacrifices superfluous.

At that time all religions had temples, places where God was near. Christian faith knows no earthly temple. The whole world is the temple of God. Jesus has gone through this temple of God and disappeared into God's mystery, into the Holy of Holies itself. And not only the whole world but every human being is a temple of God. Jesus takes up his abode with each person, there to reach the innermost depths, where we can no longer see into ourselves.

All religions and rites are governed by a compulsion to repeat rites. They must all be repeated precisely. This is also true in some high church liturgies. But where the church is reformed according to God's word, this repetition is done away with. There one can discuss whether one may or should or wants to do things differently.

Growing up and maturing in the faith through a better understanding of faith is a great task above all for Christians at a university. This task is so great that it can make us afraid. Aren't people always immature in their faith? Doesn't something childlike always remain in it? That childlike element may remain. We are to retain the trust that children have in life. But it must be a trust which has been put to the test, a trust which is up to the tasks and harshness of life. Otherwise we will become adult Christians who may have grey hairs but inwardly remain howling babies. In that case we aren't adult heirs of the promise, but immature heirs who are still in their minority.

But how do we attain such maturity of faith? The Letter to the Hebrews says that Christ is the forerunner and pioneer of *faith*. A childlike faith in a good sense is an original courage to live, trust in the goodness of life. But mature faith is a courage to live which has been tested by crises, which is crucified and risen with Christ, which with him has crossed the whole world, its depths and heights – and which has now found a firm anchor in God, where Christ now is.

The Letter to the Hebrews also says that *hope* is a sign of mature faith – a hope which doesn't make people dull and lazy. Those who have found a 'firm anchor' in God could comfortably lean back and content themselves with the certainty that all will turn out well in the end. However, that is not what is meant. What is meant is a hope which leads us to set out on the long march through the wilderness of life and never lose sight of the goal. What is meant is an activating hope.

Finally, the Letter to the Hebrews says that *love* is a sign of a mature faith. Where we feel in us the urge to love – simply the desire to help – we are on the right way. But where faith leads to lovelessness, indeed even to fanaticism, to excluding others who do not have the right faith, the disparagement of Catholics, Muslims and atheists, we are on the wrong way.

The Need to Grow in Faith

So let the Letter to the Hebrews encourage you to grow and mature in faith. That never ends throughout our lives, even when we have reached the age of fifty, sixty or seventy.

And may the peace of God which surpasses all our understanding keep your hearts and minds in Christ Jesus. Amen.

This sermon was given at the Wednesday morning service in St Peter's Church, Heidelberg on 27 October 1993. While writing it, I could hear in my head the words of an older engineer who was once again studying theology: 'Unfortunately university theology shatters the childlike faith that one brought to it.' On the other side I had read some articles on developmental theology and religious education in M. Böhnke, K.H. Reich and L. Ridez, *Erwachsene im Glauben. Beiträge zum Verhältnis von Entwicklungspsychologie und religiöses Erwachsenenbildung*, Stuttgart, Berlin and Cologne 1992.

Trust

The hidden presence of God in our life

(Hebrews 10.35)

Therefore do not throw away your trust, which has a great reward.

Human beings do not live by bread alone, but by trust. Civilized people have learned not to throw bread away. The same goes for trust. Trust is vitally important. We notice that when we meet people whose trust has collapsed.

There are people who have lost trust in their own bodies, although they are organically healthy. For them a cough is a symptom of inflammation of the lungs, flatulence a symptom of intestinal cancer, a heartbeat a symptom of a heart attack. This is known as hypochondria, and it is difficult to heal.

There are people who have lost trust in order. Before they leave home they have to check whether all the doors are closed: not just once but twice, three or four times. They fight against the chaos which threatens them everywhere with obsessive actions.

Or there are people who can't trust other men and women. When they see two others talking, they think, 'They're talking about me.' When they see two others laughing, they think, 'They're laughing at me. Everyone's on the watch to get at me.' That's called paranoid thinking.

But even when we're free of such problems, we all know at least one situation in which our trust collapses, the nightmare. I sometimes have a nightmare. I'm about to take a service, perhaps a wedding. But I've forgotten my gown. I can't find the text of my sermon. The congregation is getting restless. At least the organist could play some music, but he's disappeared. I go to the church door and the bride isn't there either. Then I wake up bathed in sweat.

Dear people, now we're all here and I can see how much trust we had in coming. The bride is here. The bridegroom is here. The organist is playing the organ. The church isn't falling down. Yet none of this can be taken for granted. Some people who would like to have come aren't here. Some people who believed that they couldn't come nevertheless have come.

Perhaps some of you are thinking, 'But the world isn't a nightmare. It's just there, and doesn't collapse into chaos. One only has to wake up and open one's eyes.' That's true. But it isn't as simple as that. I want to demonstrate this by a Buddhist story, the story of the gatekeeper.

A gatekeeper was appointed in a city to guard the city door. One day a stranger came and asked, 'What are the people in this city like? I want to settle in it.' The gatekeeper asked in return, 'What were the people like in your home town?' 'Well,' said the stranger, 'they were envious and quarrelsome.' The gatekeeper replied, 'That's what they're like here.'

Soon afterwards another stranger came with the same question. The gatekeeper asked him, too, about the people in his home town. 'Oh,' said the stranger, 'they've always been friendly and helpful.' Then the wise gatekeeper said, 'So are the people here.'

A friend who had overheard the two conversations asked, 'How can you pass such different judgments on the citizens in our city?' The gatekeeper replied, 'People are good and bad. They can be friendly and hostile, helpful and unheeding. The important thing is how one addresses them. So why should I expect these two strangers to have different experiences in our city from those they had at home? If they trust people they will find them trustworthy. And if they mistrust them, they will find them hostile.'

We have all entered this world as if it were a strange city. If we enter it with the expectation that we may trust in it, then we will find it more positive than if we mistrust it. Those who have much experience in listening to sermons will know, and the less experienced will guess, that I'm talking about faith and God here.

God is all that gives us trust. As a rule we hardly notice this, any more than we notice the air that we breathe. It surrounds us, it enters us, it lives in us, we live in it, we live through it. One can also say all this of God: God surrounds us, we live in him, live through him; he lives in us. Faith consists in our becoming conscious of this: in our giving the great conversation of life with itself a voice in us, our own voice, and in our pledging ourselves not to scorn and throw away all that gives trust in us and around us. We enter this world and say to the gatekeeper, 'I don't know the people in this city. There are good ones and bad ones among them. But I trust that I shall keep finding good people – and I myself want to be a good person for whom others who have entered this city wait and hope.' This trust is God's hidden presence in our lives.

Sometimes two people meet in this city and want to stay together for ever, like this couple. They want to express publicly that they belong together. And they want to do it before God, in that area which no public reaches. I want to play the role of the gatekeeper who gives them a word on their way, 'Don't throw away your trust.' Here are three variations on the marriage text.

First, 'Don't throw your trust *in yourself* away.' Anyone who promises a partner 'I'll stand by you for better or for worse' is also speaking for the person he or she will become in five, ten or twenty years. And one thing is certain: in five, ten or twenty years that person will no longer be what he or she now is. Trust in oneself means that one trusts to be able to stand by this promise through all the changes in life – and not because one will remain the same. On the contrary, this trust in oneself presupposes that one is going to change. Here's an illustration. We all know the school examination which consists in continuing a story which has already begun. The teacher is testing whether pupils have understood the genre of the story properly. An adventure story doesn't end in the same way as a love story. A ghost story doesn't end in the same way as a fairy tale. Today two people are pledging to continue together a story which they have already begun together. They don't yet know the continuation. There are many possible ways of continuing the story. And there are many unknown factors in it. But they are confident of being able to preserve the genre: this love story will not become a horror story. They assure us that they believe this, too. However, if they are to give the story a good ending in the great book of life they must keep developing and changing, like the characters in a novel. And this includes the trust of each individual in himself or herself. Don't throw this trust away. You're not alone here. God is a power to change, a power to convert; in this power we sense God's hidden presence in our lives.

My second variation on this marriage text is, 'Don't throw your trust *in each other* away.' I recently heard of a couple who had been living together for ten years and now wanted to marry. Before the wedding the woman confided to her partner that five years previously for a short time she had had a relationship with another man. She wanted to tell him this so that their own relationship was based on honesty and to reassure him that she was sorry about this. It wouldn't happen again. Her partner was so annoyed that he broke off the relationship. I admire this woman. There is nothing so difficult as to say, 'I made a mistake. I'm sorry with all my heart.' It is sad that her partner didn't have the strength to meet trust with trust. Perhaps he had experienced earlier how such trust can be misused; so no one should condemn him. Trust can't be put on trial. Trust is a great gift. We all know that no partnership is successful without a readiness to forgive – in things great and small. Every partnership lives by this trust. But this trust can be thrown away and misused in two ways. First, if one refuses apologies and forgiveness where they are honestly asked for. And also if apologies and forgiveness are calculated in advance. How many husbands have shamelessly exploited the readiness of their wives to forgive them? So once again, 'Don't throw your trust in each other away.' It's precious. It is God's hidden presence in your lives.

And finally my third variation on the marriage text is, 'Don't throw trust in trust away.' That sounds abstract, but what I mean is this. You can't create trust as you can build a house, make a car or write a book. Trust comes about spontaneously. It's a sovereign expression of life. It often wins through over our mistrust. Many people have experienced how members of their family lose their freedom to make contact with one another, how partnerships fail or how trust is abused. All that leaves behind scratches and wounds. Nevertheless, in the face of such experiences people keep gaining a new trust which proves more powerful than all the hurts. We can't create such trust any more than we can create the world. But we can destroy it. We can throw it away. We can't create the air by which we live either. But we can pollute it. It's the same with trust. We can destroy it through emotional smog. But just as we trust that the air will constantly renew itself, that the world will go on existing, that the nightmares in which nothing functions any longer are wrong, so we trust that trust will continue to be established spontaneously. In this constant renewal of trust we detect God's hidden presence in our life.

Dear people, my three variations on the marriage text are addressed not only to this couple but to everyone – whether you are married or married, separated or unseparated, young or old, healthy or sick, happy or unhappy. To all of you I want to appeal, 'Don't throw your trust away.' I'm aware that in many people it has been shaken. Today in particular perhaps some people are feeling disappointment, loneliness, in watching a couple celebrating their relationship. But look around again: today two people are renewing their covenant with each other, with life and with God. Today they are assuring us that trust is possible. Don't throw it away! And what could be better on such a day than for a tiny spark of trust also to begin to flicker and burn in those who came with sorrow or mixed feelings?

We all enter life every day as into a big city. And we keep passing a gatekeeper and he reminds us, 'If you enter the city with mistrust, it will quickly become a nightmare. But if you enter it with trust and faith, you will find trust.'

And if you ask, 'But aren't the wicked in this city far more powerful than the good?', then as one of the many small gate-keepers to this city I must tell you something – and it sums up all the Bible tells us as the word of God. The architect of this city has taken a great step towards helping you too to cope with this problem. He has created *you* to bring some good into this city. He has created this couple to venture on life together. He has created their child so that it may grow up full of trust with them. And he has created this day for everyone to rejoice in.

And may the peace of God which surpasses all our understanding keep your hearts and minds in Christ Jesus. Amen.

A marriage sermon given in St John's Church, Heidelberg-Neunheim on 17 May 1997. The Buddhist story about the gatekeeper can be found under the title, 'How One Calls into the Forest', in U. Tworuschka, *Himmel ist überall. Geschichten aus den Weltreligionen*, GTB 760, Gütersloh 1985, 17f.

Heaven Perplexed

And the key to the Book of Life

(Revelation 5.1–10)

And I saw in the right hand of him who was seated on the throne a scroll written inside and outside, sealed with seven seals; and I saw a strong angel proclaiming with a loud voice, 'Who is worthy to open the scroll and break its seals?' But no one in heaven or on earth or under the earth was able to open the scroll or to look into it. And I wept much that no one was found worthy to open the scroll or to look into it. Then one of the elders said to me, 'Do not weep! Look, the Lion of the tribe of Judah, the Root of David, has conquered, so that he can open the scroll and its seven seals.' And between the throne and the four living creatures and among the elders, I saw a Lamb standing, as though it had been slain, with seven horns and with seven eyes, which are the seven spirits of God sent out into all the earth; and he went and took the scroll from the right hand of him who was seated on the throne. And when he had taken the scroll, the four living creatures and the twenty-four elders fell down before the Lamb, each holding a harp, and with golden bowls full of incense, which are the prayers of the saints. And they sang a new song, saying, 'You are worthy to take the scroll and to open its seals, for you were slain and by your blood you ransomed people for God from every tribe and tongue and people and nation, and have made them a kingdom and priests to our God, and they shall reign on earth.'

Let's imagine that a state is in crisis. Everyone is perplexed. An ordinary citizen succeeds in penetrating to the centre of power, where decisions are made and trends are set. He has access to all the cabinet meetings. How shattered he would be if he found out that there too, perplexity reigns! Even there no one knows what to do next.

That is the situation of the prophet who wrote the Revelation of John. There was a great crisis in his time. The communities were expecting persecution and oppression. This had already begun in individual cases. In this situation, in his imagination the prophet penetrates to the centre of world government. He sees God himself. Now at last he wants to get the key to the riddles of world history. Now he wants the answer to so many questions. Why must the righteous suffer? Why does misfortune strike the innocent, the children? And what does he discover in heaven? There too people are perplexed. There too people don't know what to do next.

The riddles of the world, history and life appear in our text as a book with seven seals. It is closed, inaccessible. The heavenly government looks for someone who can open it and read it. An angel calls out, 'Who is worthy and capable of opening the book, of breaking its seals? Who will give an answer to the questions which torment human beings?' He calls into the void. For no one in heaven, no one on earth, no one under the earth is capable of opening the book. No one knows an answer to the great riddles of the world.

The prophet can't understand it. He collapses. He weeps. For a moment everything seems to him to be vain and meaningless. If even in heaven no one has access to the riddles of the world, then they will remain unsolved for ever.

Had the angel asked us people of the twentieth century, 'Who is capable of reading the book?', we would probably have made three suggestions.

Our first suggestion might have been that a Nobel prize-winner in the natural sciences should decipher the book of the world. I can already see in my mind's eye a distinguished old gentleman with white hair appearing before the heavenly council. And he says, 'Yes, we're looking for the great world formula, for a unity behind all the forces of nature. We're deciphering the book of nature. We're showing how it organized itself into ever new forms – until it brought forth us human beings on a tiny planet on the periphery of one of the many Milky Way systems – us, the first living beings who are attempting to read the book of nature. But the more we read and read, the more uncertain we become about our own role in this book. Were we foreseen at all? Is it perhaps unimportant that we exist?' The conclusion of the natural scientist is that while we can read the book of nature, we don't know what human beings are doing in it. He might add, 'Perhaps we shall learn that not from nature, but from history.'

So a second suggestion would be that a politician should decipher the book of history. He should say what we human beings should be doing, what direction we should take. But however hard people look for a politician, none appears. Politicians don't trust themselves. No wonder they don't have a good reputation at the present time! They're concerned to keep on top, with their rivals underneath them and strangers outside. They don't know what the trend is. Nor would we expect too much of them. That would be unfair. But even if they had an answer, there is a book that they certainly can't decipher, the book of each person's own quite personal, irreplaceable, individual life. That can be read only by the individual concerned.

So a third proposal is that this book of one's own life should be read by a monk from East Asia. And I can already see one of these friendly figures approaching. His face radiates peace. He says, 'The key for opening the book lies in you yourself. Know yourself. See through your self. It's unreal, an illusion. Learn to let go of yourself. Set yourself free, like a balloon which rises to heaven and is dissolved in it. I can't decipher the book of nature, of history or even of your own life for you. But I can teach you to let go of the wish to decipher all these books. Then you will have peace, when you've overcome the thirst for life, for understanding, for deciphering the book.'

Dear people, you will certainly have noticed that today also it's true that no one in heaven, or on earth or under the earth can open the book: no Nobel prize-winner, no politician, no monk from East Asia. But the prophet of the Revelation of John has an answer. He has heard a voice which says, 'There is one who can open this book. He comes from Israel. He is not a winner in world history but a loser. He is not powerful. He is a lamb which has been slaughtered. Only Jesus can open the book of the seven seals.' That is the message of the text.

But how does Jesus open the threefold book for us: the book of nature, of history and of our own lives? Let's listen to the hymn of praise to him:

You are worthy, our Lord and our God . . .
for you have made all things,
through your will they were and have been created.

Here we hear the words, 'You are worthy.' They refer to God. And we ask ourselves: why isn't God also worthy to open the book? Why does he need the lamb to write the book of creation to the end? And why does he need a slaughtered lamb?

This question is a fundamental one for theology. I've kept reflecting on it for many years, and this is the answer that I've found. This one sacrificial lamb replaces bloody sacrifices. For centuries human beings had sacrificed animals. They regarded that as the most important thing in their worship. Why? Why this slaughtering of other life to the greater glory of the gods? Why did people think that the world would collapse if they no longer sacrificed? I suspect that our ancestors knew better than we do that all life lives at the expense of other life. So they sacrificed other life in order to safeguard and enhance their own. To the present day we live at the expense of other living beings. We are displacing them from the earth. Many species are dying out. We rear many animals, only to slaughter them and eat them. And yet we know that all life is deeply related. It's like a part of ourselves. When we live at the expense of other life, we are living in a split from ourselves.

The lamb that was slaughtered sets this split with ourselves before our eyes. But it overcomes it. Through its existence it assures us that there is a life which doesn't live at the expense of other life, a life in which the weaker isn't sacrificed for the stronger, a life in which people sacrifice something of themselves in favour of those who are weaker. That is the message of the lamb.

Albert Schweitzer heard this message when he was studying the New Testament. He obeyed it when he went into the primeval forest to help people there who were marked by suffering. He had found the role which God assigns us in the overall context of things: to extend his creation beyond nature as it has been so far so that already today, symbolically and by way of a beginning, a life can start in which the strong no longer live at the expense of the weak.

Secondly, let's take the book of history into which our politicians so want to enter their deeds. The sealed book of the Revelation of John is also in one respect a political book. When the angels praise God as 'our Lord and our God', that is a protest against the Roman empire Domitian. For he was the first emperor to call himself 'lord and god'. In his time Christians were persecuted because they refused to call a human being 'god'. The politics of the lamb is a protest against any politics which makes the ruler or the state absolute and divinizes them.

This lamb is praised because it brings together people 'from every tribe and tongue and people and nation'. Whereas our politicians and many others today are concerned with keeping other people out, deterring asylum-seekers, refugees and immigrants, the lamb creates a community of many peoples. So don't believe those who want to persuade us once again today that there are insuperable differences between nations and cultures, that the others are different. The Christian community is proof to the contrary. There are Chinese, Japanese, Indian, African and Brazilian Christians. There are Christians in every people, on every continent, in every culture. Is there a better indication that there need be no insuperable differences between peoples and cultures? And don't we Christians have the special task of making people aware of that? No religion is present in so many different nations world-wide today – usually only as a minority, and in many areas of our country only as a minority. But we are a minority which is everywhere.

Now what does Jesus do in his community of people from the many races and nations? Does he make them asylum-seekers who are tolerated? No, our text says, he makes them 'kings and priests for God'. Then follows the amazing statement, 'And they will reign on earth.' All are to be kings, all are to be priests. And Christians said that when faced by an emperor who in principle wanted to set himself up over all others. They said to him, 'We Christians, we little people, are already kings through Jesus. You too are only a human being like us.'

The book with the seven seals which is opened by the lamb says where history is going to. We shall come to the point when all human beings become kings, when all can experience that they are of infinite value, and no one oppresses others and regards himself as more than human.

But the book with seven seals is not only the book of nature and history. It is also the book of your life. Only one person is worthy and capable of reading it, and that is you. No one else can do it in your place. But perhaps you will say, 'I don't understand myself. My life is so muddled and confused that it doesn't make sense.' Perhaps you will say that there are many chapters in the book of your life which are so painful that you don't even want to read them. And perhaps a chapter is beginning for you which you would much prefer to skip: a sad chapter, a chapter in which there will be much about sickness, separation and death.

Isn't the friendly monk from East Asia right when he says, 'Your self is an illusion! Detach yourself from it. There's no sense in it. You're tormenting yourself in vain with your questions'? But however seductive the answer may be for many people, the Christian answer is different. In the Revelation of John Jesus says:

'Behold, I stand at the door and knock;
if anyone hears my voice
and opens the door,
I will come in to him
and hold eucharist with him' (3.20).

If Jesus enters your life, if through him God becomes present in your life, then you aren't an illusion. Then you're a dwelling-place of God. Then you're a temple of God. Then you're infinitely valuable, even if so much has gone wrong in your life. Then you're a section in the book of God. And you may not only read it, but write it to the end.

Therefore today I ask you also to write the history of Jesus into the book of your life. Then you will read your own history with other eyes. You will still read much that is alien and painful in the book of your life. But you needn't be ashamed of it. You will read that sometimes you were a perpetrator and sometimes a victim. You were pushed away by others, but sometimes you also pushed others away. And you were to blame. But when you inscribe the story of Jesus in the book of your life, you will be given the certainty that you are forgiven. You will often go on doubting and despairing because of the sorry chapters in your life and ask yourself whether there is any meaning in it. When you do, remember the angel in the Revelation of John. He asked, 'Who is worthy and capable of opening and reading the sealed book?' Who is capable of deciphering the book of nature, history and your life? It is still true that no one can really do this, not even in heaven. Even heaven is dependent on the lamb to open the sealed book, to give an answer to the insoluble question: Why does misfortune strike the innocent? Why do even children suffer? An answer can be given only by someone who himself has suffered inno-cently. You won't find a better answer even in heaven.

If you write the history of Jesus into the book of your life, then it will become a good history. And when it has been written to the end, you may put the book of your life back in God's hands. You remain a section in God's great book. And none of it will be lost.

And may the peace of God, which surpasses all our under-standing, keep your hearts in Christ Jesus. Amen.

Heaven Perplexed

This sermon was given on the First Sunday in Advent, 29 November 1993, in Sexau, in connection with the award of the Sexau Community Prize for Theology; it was first published in G. Theissen, *Frauen im Umfeld Jesus*, Sexau Gemeindepreis für Theologie 11, Sexau 1993, 24–32.